S0-BOA-468

ENCOUNTERS

POETIC
MEDITATIONS
ON THE
OLD TESTAMENT

by

J. Barrie Shepherd

The Pilgrim Press
New York

Copyright © 1983 The Pilgrim Press
All rights reserved

No part of this publication may be reproduced, stored in a
retrieval system, or transmitted in any form or by any means,
electronic, mechanical, photocopying, recording, or
otherwise (brief quotations used in magazines or newspaper
reviews excepted), without the prior permission of the
publisher.

Library of Congress Cataloging in Publication Data

Shepherd, J. Barrie.
    Encounters: poetic meditations on the
Old Testament.

    1. Bible. O. T.—Meditations.   I. Title.
BS1151.5.S53   1983   242'.5   82-22422
ISBN 0-8298-0637-7 (pbk.)

Scripture quotations, unless otherwise indicated, are from the
Revised Standard Version of the Bible, copyright 1946, 1952
and © 1971 by the Division of Christian Education, National
Council of Churches, and are used by permission. Scripture
quotations marked KJV are from the *King James Version*. The
scripture quotation noted as PHILLIPS is from *The New
Testament in Modern English* by J.B. Phillips (New York:
Macmillan Publishing House). © J.B. Phillips 1958, 1960,
1972. The scripture quotation marked NEB is from *The New
English Bible* © The Delegates of the Oxford University Press
and The Syndics of the Cambridge University Press, 1961,
1970. Reprinted by permission.

The Pilgrim Press, 132 West 31 Street, New York, NY 10001

Louise Jones

ENCOUNTERS

Other books by J. Barrie Shepherd
Diary of Daily Prayer
A Diary of Prayer

I dedicate this book in gratitude to the congregation of the Swarthmore Presbyterian Church, whose encouragement and critical support have played a major role in its creation

CONTENTS

FOREWORD

The voice (the mind, the pen, the typewriter) of Barrie Shepherd is an uncommon, even rare, possession of the church in our time. In him and in his ministry are combined the qualities essential to authentically distinguished preaching—sophisticated, contemporary knowledge of the Bible; sensitivity at once to what the biblical story *was* and what it *is*; a profound and/or delicate awareness of where we all are in the life of faith; an intelligent, courageous commitment to the gospel and the life of the church, which it forms and nourishes; and withal a superb, highly gifted use of language.

If the words of these verse-sermon-essays are inspired, so is the selection—and in some cases even juxtaposition—of biblical texts around and upon which the author moves us, instructs us, convicts us, disturbs us—and always reminds us that we are in any ultimate sense forgiven, loved, and redeemed. The very *choice* of texts enhances the power of the biblical Word, and the Shepherd word, to find us where we are and to make that story contemporary with ours, or ours with it.

It is trite to say that I picked up this collection of lyrical biblical commentaries and could not easily put it down. But it is true. And you will find it so; and as you read and when you are done, you will know that the biblical Word has come home to you, never to leave you quite the same.

Davie Napier

PREFACE

Many of the incidents or "Encounters" treated in this book may seem rather familiar, even "old hat," to the biblically literate reader, having been examined and expounded at regular intervals by generations of preachers and biblical scholars. Two considerations have encouraged me to make yet another attempt upon this ancient material.

The first is based on my hope that the approach I have taken, with its use of poetry and sympathetic imagination, will open up occasional new insights and new perspectives into meaning; or, failing this, will at the least refresh and renew interest in these timeworn yet still potentially revealing narratives. My second consideration arises from the observation that the assumption—above—of the biblically literate reader has become more and more dubious. Not only in my personal experience of eighteen years of ministry—on the campus, in college teaching, and in the parish—but also in the testimony of colleagues and in reports from the church at large, the realization appears to be spreading that we are living and serving today in a biblically deprived generation.

The classic parables and tales of valor, even such old favorites as the Sermon on the Mount and the Decalogue, are no longer standard issue for the educational equipment of the mind. Instead they tend to be added on, if at all, as extras or frills, depending on the preference or whim of the individual teacher. Therefore it may well be that an imaginative retelling of these dramatic episodes from our tradition will prove to be not only helpful but even overdue.

It should be made clear at the outset that the full impact of these chapters will be felt only if the reader has first taken the trouble to study the text of the biblical incident in question. Indeed, in several cases the content of the chapter may be almost incomprehensible without such a reading. Each chapter begins with a key or thematic text and a reference to the entire scriptural passage to be reviewed.

Finally, a word about consistency. At times the messages of specific "Encounters" within this book may appear to be in conflict with one another. Such "contradictions" are hardly a novel experience in the study of the scriptures. The goal here is to be not too tightly bound by the narrow requirements of consistency, but rather to permit each "Encounter" to speak for itself and thus to derive from this entire series of divine-human experiences a richer, fuller conception of the relationship between the Creator and the human creation. Such a conception will not necessarily prove to be more manageable, more logical, more systematic. The book presents a series of vignettes, scenes of God in action with God's people. If it ends by making our image of God less sharp and precisely defined than heretofore, so be it. That is one reason for ending with the mysterious vision of Ezekiel and the Wheel. It is my hope that, while the resulting image may be less clearly delineated, it will also be more comprehensive and more true to life—life which, when honestly observed, has never proved to be all that logical or consistent.

ENCOUNTERS

Chapter One
Genesis 32

JACOB
AT JABBOK

> The sun rose upon [Jacob]
> as he passed Penuel,
> limping because of his thigh.
> —Genesis 32:31

The scenario is hardly unique.
We can catch it any fall or winter Sunday,
many evenings on the tube
as the battered, mudstained athlete
hobbles slowly from the field.
Exhaustion blends with agony taut
across his handsome face,
and something seems decidedly amiss
with the functioning of one of his legs.
Attentive coaches scurry to assist him home.
Commentators build the level of anxiety
among the troubled fans until
(relief!) the reassuring word is passed,
"Only a muscle spasm . . .
fit to take the field again next week."
And attention turns again
with quickened appetite to the mayhem
in the middle of the gridiron.

Yet, as Jacob drags his weary self
across our line of inner vision, the limp
may seem familiar, but the setting
certainly is not. Here is no giant stadium,
floodlights, grandstands, cheering crowds,
but a solitary river bank, the sunrise for a backdrop.
Here we have no tall and trim young athlete-hero,
but a middle-aged fellow
with gray in his beard, a bulge
at his belt line and two wives with eleven children
anxiously awaiting his return.

A weird tale this, of Jacob at Jabbok,
an uncanny, untidy narrative, full of loose ends,
questions, problems. Hardly "biblical"
as one would have imagined stories from a holy book.
What is going on here, anyway?
What, in the first place, was Jacob doing
all alone by that river at night?
What was the dread significance of daybreak,
or of touching Jacob's thigh?
And what is all this business of new names
and not eating the sinew of the hip?

Three questions in particular
capture the mystery and meaning of this tale.
Three questions of the wrestling match at Jabbok.
The first is this: Who is wrestling
with this man? Who *is* this wrestling with Jacob?

Set yourself in Jacob's sandals
for a moment. You are returning
after many years of exile, years in which
you have prospered vastly at the expense
of your father-in-law, Laban,
years in which you have almost forgotten,
but not quite, how you cheated, long ago,
your own brother, rough and ready, hairy Esau,
of the inheritance of Isaac, almost
forgotten how you fled
in peril of your life into the wilderness
to camp and see within a dream
the steps of angels moving
to and from the Presence.

Now, back at the border once again,
you hear that your twin brother with a force
of some four hundred men approaches rapidly.
A flash of the old panic re-ignites.
You push ahead of you great gifts, envoys
of peace, even your own wives,
Leah, Rachel, and the children,
to intercede on your behalf.
Then settle down to sleep, if possible,
beside the stream.

Suddenly, out of the dark, a strange assailant
grasps you by the throat.
Esau!
Surely that is your first thought
as you gasp for breath and claw away
to break the cruel, choking grip. Esau,
come ahead, alone, to seek revenge
as man to man. But as you grapple in the silence
and the sweat of pitch-black night
a wilder, far more fearsome thought begins to dawn—
this is no human power you wrestle with.
A devil then, the spirit of the Jabbok
springing up like vapors of the night
to contest the crossing with you.
You struggle even harder, straining to prevail
when, just as the new day starts to break,
you are flung to the ground
with the dawning realization that . . . My God!
this is neither man nor demon, neither bogeyman
nor brother that you strain against,
have battled with the long night through.
You have been clinging to,
contending with the Holy One,
Almighty God!

What can this mean,
for then, for now, for each
and every now?
At least the struggle
should not seem too unfamiliar.
We all have known, still know from day
to day this sense of life as one long
never-ending wrestling match,
no rules, no referee.
We struggle for a living
making ends meet in these hard and testing times.
We grapple with competitors,
brother Esaus in a sense; all those others
who would grasp the same fruits we seek, who race
against us for the sweet, if swiftly passing, prizes
of this eager world.

We struggle against demons too,
at least, might call them demons, those powers
within, about us, that reach out claws to grip us,
drag us down to laziness or apathy, to lust
or careless living, to quick and easy,
sleazy ways to make a buck or get ahead
or merely stay afloat. Yes, we know
just what it's like to spend our days and nights
in one colossal struggle.

But a wrestling match with *God*?
Surely God is one who blesses us, who cares
for us, binds up our hurts and wounds,
not cripples us, destroys us.
Whom *do* we struggle with, however,
most of the time? Do we really, truly wage
war against sin and evil? Or do we wrestle more,
much more, against the will of God,
the love of God?
Is it not true to say, for many,
that at the very core of our conflict
there is not so much the cosmic clash of good and evil,
rather that more timid tussle
to find ways around the ways of God,
to substitute for love the cozier paths
of fear and self-protection.
"Preserve us. O preserve us against love!"
is our cry. "Love costs too much. Couldn't we
just get by with a little charity
here and there, the odd good deed
to make us feel at ease without
having to plunge all the way
into love?"

So we know whom Jacob wrestled with
at Jabbok, for, at the deepest level
of our lives, our souls,
we share that struggle with him.
We too are all-too-frantic
to avoid the grace of God.

8

> The sun rose upon Jacob
> as he passed Penuel,
> limping because of his thigh.

Who is wrestling with this man? And now,
the second question: Why is this man limping?
We don't think much of limpers
in this healthy world of ours.
It is true that, of late,
we have become a little more concerned,
have passed new laws and built new ramps
to accommodate the handicapped.
But all of this is still conceived as charity,
as kindness, as a favor we bestow, when
and if we can afford it.
We don't think much of limpers
in this fierce world of ours. Just try
calling someone a "cripple."
Then, I think, you'll catch my meaning.

Yet here is Jacob;
Jacob, the bright, shiny new embodiment
of all the hope and promise in God's plan,
Jacob rising totally renewed,
transformed even to the extent of a new name
by this transfiguring encounter with his God,
and he strides into the new day
with a limp.
Just what might be the meaning,
the profound, theological,
relating-to-your-life-and-mine meaning
of that limp?

9

The television preachers, for the most part,
those mass-marketed media gospeleers,
will tell you that those
whose lives are close to God, those who
have felt God's powerful, conquering, renewing
touch of love within their heart of hearts
can throw away their crutches.
Our friendly God removes
all our problems, all our pains,
or so they claim. "God blesses those
God loves with radiant health and strength,
prosperity and all things sweet and pleasant
to the eye, the ear, the taste."
"Material wealth, success with all its trappings,
these are merely clear and certain signs that
I am on the Lord's team and the Lord,
of course, is on mine."
Such is their glittering message!
And it has its plausibility, to be sure.
After all, should not we Christians,
soldiers of the risen Christ, stride in
triumph, glowing, healthy, glistening
with success through all the trials
and tribulations of this world?
Why, then, why are so many
of us still limping?

10

In the other camp,
we hear the cynic's sneer,
"The church is just a crutch,"
a place where all the halt and maimed
take refuge from the rigors of this life
because they cannot stand the pace.
And we want to say, "This too is true,
yet who is there can walk this life
we lead today and not begin to limp?"
So Jacob rose and entered into
his new day bearing a decided limp.

> The sun rose upon Jacob
> as he passed Penuel,
> limping because of his thigh.

Why is this man,
why are we all limping?
Can it be this love of God
must wound us so that it can heal us?
Might this halting hip of Jacob signify
that when we do contend with love, when we
grapple with and finally are transformed by
the power of God's grace we become
more vulnerable, not less;
more likely to get hurt than
those who choose always to play it safe,
protect themselves from contact with the world,
deny the risky call to caring?

11

Might that Galilean have been serious,
deadly serious, when he said that to come
after him meant taking up a cross?
Is being wounded part of being open, caring,
giving, sharing, loving? Could it be that
within the holy commonwealth of grace
the one who limps bears not a handicap,
no stigma, but a medal, badge of honor?

> The sun rose upon Jacob
> as he passed Penuel,
> limping because of his thigh.

Who is wrestling with this man?
Why is this man limping? And one further question:
What is this man's name?
What is he to be called, this one
who struggles, wrestles to the death
and life with God, the love that God is
and that is our God?
The story calls him Israel,
or rather *Yisra-el*, the one who strives with God.

And so he was, and is. The people Israel
have lived for twenty, thirty centuries the pain
mixed with the blessing of being
vulnerable to and for Yahweh.
The church as well, this second Israel
in Christ, has known and knows today
the same experience in Korea and Taiwan,
in Poland, South America,
in places all across this globe
where faithful persons suffer for their faith.

His name is Israel;
but his name is also Bill and Pat and Susan,
Don and Carol and a multitude of others,
all who suffer yet are faithful to the end.
Above all he bears the name
of one who also limped
with bruised and bloodstained,
broken feet across the threshold of a garden tomb
into the sunrise of an Easter dawn
and on into our hearts and lives forever.

For Jacob-Yisrael
in this odd, uncanny incident
beside the brook of Jabbok foreshadows much,
very much that is to come,
lends meaning, even here today
to the struggling, the suffering we share,
to the new and full identity
that comes to us in Jesus Christ.

Then let us struggle *for* the love
of God and not against it. Let us be wounded,
vulnerable, open to the blows that come
through sharing love in Christ's name.
Let us recognize and live
our wounds and hurts for what they truly are,
the symbols of God's love at work,
the first and early signs
of the dawning of God's everlasting kingdom.

> The sun rose upon Jacob
> as he passed Penuel,
> limping because of his thigh.

Chapter Two
Exodus 2—3

MOSES
ON THE MOUNTAIN

"If I come to the people of Israel and say to them,
'The God of your fathers has sent me to you,'
and they ask me, 'What is his name?'
what shall I say to them?"
God said to Moses, "I AM WHO I AM."
—Exodus 3:13

This question rings a bell,
a bell that echoes back one chapter
or perhaps three hundred years to Jacob
wrestling at Jabbok with the "Lord of Hosts" by night
and asking, "Tell me, I pray, your name."
What *is* your name, O God? What on earth
are we to call you?

So we see Moses,
former prince of Pharaoh's house
now fugitive, a wanted man,
the killer of an overseer who beat a Hebrew slave;
Moses, who is now, it would appear,
quite cozily ensconced
in a whole new way of life,
lovely young wife, Zipporah,
prosperous and helpful in-laws,
flocks and herds to tend
out in the peaceful, solitary wilderness;

Moses, suddenly and somewhat rudely reawakened
to the dreadful situation of his own,
his folk in Egypt, reawakened by the presence
of the Holy One of Israel
calling to him from the burning
yet unburning bush,

Exodus 3:7, 10

"I have seen the affliction of my people . . .
and have heard their cry . . . ;
I know their sufferings. . . .
Come, I will send you to Pharaoh
that you may bring forth my people."

And Moses said to God,
"Who is calling? Who shall I say sent me?
Tell me, I pray, your name."
Yes, the question rings a bell.

What is the name of God?
Or better yet, Why did they,
why do we need to know God's name?
To know a name is to hold power, power over someone.
If I know your name I can call you,
call upon you, classify you, put you on a list,
use your label as a handle to control.
I can slander you behind your back,
support you, promote your cause
if I only know your name.

16

A stranger approaches,
someone you have never seen before,
source, therefore, of possible threat
or of potential benefit, someone who might
take from you or share with you.
But you have to know the name
to let that process take its course
or hold it back. So we ask,
What is your name?
The ancient world knew this,
for the name was not mere label,
contained a family, a history, a clan,
could tell you, in a moment, friend or foe.
Still more, the name, back long ago,
held something of the essence, the identity,
so that to know a name was to possess
a vital inner knowledge, power over what
or who that name denoted. To know
the name of a god, therefore,
was something truly crucial. How else to call
upon that deity, to claim it for your own,
to demand its help or guidance, to employ it
in a spell perhaps, or to place a curse
upon your foes? Hence the true and fullest
meaning of the third commandment about
taking Yahweh's name in vain.
So Moses, as Jacob long before him,
sought to know the name of God.

> "If I come to the people . . .
> and they ask me, 'What is his name?'
> what shall I say to them?"

The answer that God gave,
Ehyeh asher ehyeh—I am who I am,
or perhaps, I will be what I will be,
has been the spark of more discussion, more debate
and disagreement, than almost any other
portion of the scriptures.
What, first of all, does it mean,
Ehyeh asher ehyeh? And then,
What can that meaning tell us about God?

Translations, explanations, they are legion,
their limit only in the rich imagination of the race.
From all of these, two possibilities may serve
to glimpse, combined, what might be held
within this fuller way of saying "God."

"I am who I am" might first
be taken to express a sense of holy,
wholly otherness. "Don't try to pin me down, man!"
Or, as the old song put it, "Don't fence me in."
I am who I am—I will be what I will be
and all your attempts at definition,
clarification, systematization
are just a waste of time, indeed,
a striving after wind.

I am who I am
and when all your books are written,
all your catalogs and libraries compiled,
all your songs sung and pictures painted,
all your lectures given, sermons preached and poems
written, I will be what I will be just because
I am Yahweh—the One beyond
all systems and all creeds, the One,
the only One who is free, completely free,
bound by neither space nor time,
logic nor geometry, race nor sex,
nor species even, free to be
whatever I will be.

Thus the book of Job,
great masterpiece of faith and doubt where,
after nearly forty chapters of arguments and theories,
debates about God's justice and God's laws,
God appears in person,
says to Job, "How dare you question me?
Now I will question you and you
will answer me, O man."

We need to hear this
in our churches, our colleges,
our seminaries and our Sunday schools today.
We need to recognize that, when all is said and done,
when all our dogmas of the Trinity, the Atonement,
the Cross, when all our creeds and doctrines
are finally and fully explicated,
laid out in plan and color-coded, there still
remains the mystery that is God.

19

We need to realize,
teach our youngsters too,
that whenever we try to pin God down,
to say, "God will do this and won't do that.
God will be here, not there. God favors our side,
disfavors theirs," then we are trespassing.
We are trampling holy ground
in hobnailed hiking boots.

When Moses, you recall, approached the bush,
he took his shoes from off his feet.
When we approach the reality that is God
we too must shed all our pretensions,
all the rigid preconceptions
that have shielded from God's judgment
and God's call. We must leave off from talk entirely,
be prepared to listen, simply listen
to the voice of One who says,
"I am who I am."

> Then Moses said to God,
> "If I come to the people of Israel . . .
> and they ask me, 'What is his name?'
> what shall I say to them?"

But then, is God
complete and total mystery? Is this "Lord of hosts"
so utterly unpredictable, even worse,
so arbitrary and capricious?
Is there nothing we can know for sure,
depend on with our God?

Return now to *Ehyeh asher ehyeh*
to seek interpretation of a second kind
to contrast, balance, moderate the first.
This God who said, "My name is I Am Who I Am"
is a God who meant to emphasize
the present tense, the here-and-nowness of "I Am."
"I Am Who I Am *now*." "I am to be defined,
described, approached, named, and understood
through all this experience, this encounter
you are undergoing in this present moment."

"This, which is happening to you now,
is who I am, Moses, this is
what I will be—a mystery indeed, a holy presence
that may only be approached with naked feet
and heart and soul.
But I am also,
don't you see, God of your fathers, as I told you,
God of Abraham, Isaac, Jacob, Joseph
and therefore the One who promised blessing
to you, who has committed, covenanted to restore this
broken, soiled and torn creation working
through you. I am God of your mothers too,
of Sarah and Rebekah, Leah, Rachel,
God who led you, and your folk from long ago
through all the trials, tempests, turmoils of this
life until this very day. This
is who I am, Moses, God of your past,
of your rich tradition, of your history,
as well as of your bitter present; God of all
your hoping for the future."

"Listen further, Moses,
'I am who I am,' that means
the One who sees and hears and knows;
who sees the pain of your people,
who hears their cry for freedom,
who knows, and even shares
(for that is part of knowing in your language),
who knows-shares their anguish under Egypt
and who is come, at last, to save and
to redeem, for I love them with
an everlasting love."

"This too is who I am, Moses.
'I am who I am.'
I am therefore also this one
who summons you to turn your steps,
your life around, to forsake all this security,
go back into the land you fled from
and to serve me there with only this to strengthen,
my promise, I will be with you,
This too is who I am."

"I am who I am, Moses.
A God who does not lend
divine identity and name to abstract theories
and bloodless propositions,
but who can be known, who can be seen,
who can be touched and grasped, even held onto
in the whirlpool of events and of experience.

I am not a God to be put down on paper,
modeled with care in clay or stone,
but a God to be lived out in action and
in service, in setting captive people free.
This is also who I am, Moses.
I am who I am."

"I am who I am—I will be what I will be
and you will find me, I will be with you wherever
chains are broken, shackles of all kinds,
wherever human lives find transformation,
wherever evil is being overcome, not by greater
evil but by good, where pain is being neutralized,
loneliness and lostness being healed, wherever death,
the powers of death in all their manifold,
subtle and intricate forms are being overcome
by life and love and trust."

> Then Moses said to God,
> "If I come to the people of Israel . . .
> and they ask me, 'What is his name?'
> what shall I say to them?"

"Go tell them
yes, tell all my people everywhere,
that Egypt is far more than
any once-for-all historical event
over and done with long ago and far away.

The powers of death, those forces in you and
around you that would crush the human soul—
forces of poverty and disease, of racism, sexism,
and totalitarianism, of addiction and greed, of apathy
and despair—those forces which around the world
today pile weapon upon weapon and neglect
the ways of peace are just as real
and every bit as evil as any pharaoh
and his brutal taskmasters."

"If you would know the name of God,
if you would know the meaning and the presence
of I Am Who I Am, then you, as individuals,
as families, communities and churches
must let go of your securities and grapple with
those forces just as Moses did.
If and when you do you have my promise,
I will be with you, with you not only
as I was with Moses, but also
and more fully through the risen, conquering
presence of the One who followed Moses
to set *all* God's people free,
even Jesus Christ, my Son, your Lord."

Then Moses said to God,
"If I come to the people of Israel and say to them,
'The God of your fathers has sent me to you,'
and they ask me, 'What is his name?'
what shall I say to them?" God said to Moses,
"I AM WHO I AM."

24

Chapter Three
Exodus 3—4

ANOTHER LOOK AT MOSES

You shall be called
the repairer of the breach,
the restorer of streets to dwell in.
—Isaiah 58:12

There was another question asked
in that meeting by the bush that burned,
a question previous to Moses'
"Who are you, God?"
For Moses first of all asked,
"Who am I?"

Yahweh said,

Exodus 3:10-11

> "Come, I will send you to Pharaoh
> that you may bring forth my people. . . ."
> But Moses said to God,
> "Who am I
> that I should go to Pharaoh,
> and bring the sons of Israel out
> of Egypt?"

25

Who am I?
Do you see what Moses asks here?
Do you catch the implications of this
seemingly so modest, unassuming little question,
Who am I?
"Fine idea, God, I mean
that's really wonderful that you
are going to put an end, at last, to all
the torment of my people—your people—
under Pharaoh. An excellent,
a capital idea!
But not by means of me, Great One.
You surely can't be serious.
Not by little old me!

"Let's face it, Yahweh,
who am I to take on such a magnificent,
if, admittedly, somewhat hazardous assignment?
I don't deserve to be the liberator,
father-founder of a nation.
No, my life has been too shady,
spotty, stained and flawed by weakness,
even cowardice, so some might say.
Save this honor, God,
this clear undoubted honor, to be sure,
for someone of a higher caliber,
made of truly nobler stuff
than I can ever claim.
Who am I?

26

"Who am I, Yahweh?
Take a closer look.
Examine all my past, you'll see,
there are absolutely no credentials there,
nothing that would fit me for this
highly specialized task.
I grew up, don't you remember,
prepared to be a prince,
perhaps even a pharaoh,
but not a scheming
and intriguing politician.

"Besides all this,
the Egyptian authorities,
as I'm sure you are aware,
are most anxious to discuss with me
the minor matter of the murder
of an overseer of slaves.
If I go back to challenge them,
don't you see, then I'm a sure thing
to end up in jail for life, or some fate
even worse than that . . . . Fat lot of good
I could do then to save these
wretched people that you lay
upon my tender conscience.

"These Hebrew people too, God,
they won't trust me, don't you understand?
Why should they?
Why should these tattered remnants
and survivors raise their hopes, their
unarmed fists, their shackled feet
and follow me? They don't know me.
In everything but accident of birth I am Egyptian,
an Egyptian prince, a son, no less,
of Pharaoh's household; Pharaoh the oppressor.
So what, if I killed a taskmaster
who thrashed a Hebrew slave one day?
That was probably the settling of
a private grudge, the time and place
a mere coincidence, or so they will imagine.
They will not trust me, but suspect a trick,
a plot by Pharaoh to find cause
to execute them all.

"Oh, no! You've chosen
the wrong person this time.
It's a fine idea, really it is,
a worthy cause for someone,
but not for me. Think again, Yahweh.
Or better yet, why don't I try
to come up with a list of names,
a select group of much more likely prospects
for you? But not me, God.
Who am I?"

One of the most amazing graces
of these scriptures we call "Holy"
is their honesty, their frank, refreshing honesty.
Here is Moses,
the great lawgiver,
father of the Hebrew nation,
that towering figure of the plagues,
the exodus, the Red Sea, the commandments,
here is Moses acting just like one of us might act—
a chicken-hearted, lily-livered cop-out!
Yet here is the secret, the most
potentially explosive ingredient of
this entire Book of books; that folk like these—
a crook like Jacob, a philandering fool like David,
a blusterer like Peter, a bigot
like Paul—can be transformed, made whole,
made new by a power that is beyond
and yet within.

> You shall be called
> the repairer of the breach,
> the restorer of streets to dwell in.

And here we stand today
before, not a bush that burns,
but a whole world that seems about to burst
in flames about our heads.

The call has come,
has come to us in our own time
to be ambassadors for peace, to go
before the courts and governments,
the pharaohs of our age and tell them,
"Let my people go.
Let them go before it is
too late for peace."

The challenge rises from the church.
The call to action echoes just beneath
the headlines in the press, the nightly news
on television. It was reported just the other day
what one solitary "successful" missile
could achieve in the skies above New York.
Two-and-a-half million people
killed within an instant,

1 Corinthians 15:52

                    in a moment,
                    in the twinkling of an eye . . .

incinerated with scarcely time
to make a prayer, or even
close their eyes.

One day's harvest of headlines
ran like this:

          Bagdad Nuclear Plant Bombed
          Syria Urges Expel Israel From UN
          The Day The Titan Missile Talked
          To Block Strait Mines Or Artillery Called Best
          U.S. Gift To Saudis—Four Radar Planes For Defense

Then, right on the center page,

MacNamara Condemns U.S. Record On World Poverty

It seems that Robert MacNamara,
former Secretary of Defense, former prince
of the business and economic world at the helm
of Ford Motor Company (Pharaoh's court?),
MacNamara wept in public as he
stepped down from the post of head
of the World Bank, quoting statistics to prove
that this rich and fertile land, the U.S.A., devotes less,
in relation to its wealth, than any other
noncommunist, industrialized nation,
to the struggle against world poverty.
Eighteen one-hundredths of one percent of GNP
goes off in foreign aid as compared
to an average in the West
of some thirty-four one-hundredths
of one percent. And Yahweh said,

> You shall be called
> the repairer of the breach,
> the restorer of streets to dwell in.

"Who, me, God?
Be a peacemaker?
With all that's going on right now?
With all my other urgencies, priorities,
all those inabilities and handicaps that hold me back?

31

Now please don't get me wrong.
It's a wonderful idea. I've always believed
in peace, hoped and prayed and dreamed of peace.
But as for making peace, building it brick
by well-nigh-strawless brick,
I'm not your one. Who am I,
after all? Who am I?"

Yahweh answered Moses' question,
although it doesn't look all that much
like an answer. God actually responded to
Moses' query, Who am I?

Exodus 3:11-12

> But Moses said to God, "Who am I that
> I should go to Pharaoh, and bring the
> sons of Israel out of Egypt?" [God] said,
> "But I will be with you."

"This is who you are, Moses,
who you will be from this day forward,
not simply Moses the prince, the fugitive,
the chicken-hearted shepherd;
but Moses with whom I am—
Moses with whom God is walking."

Might we also, in this light, see who we are,
who we all are in Christ Jesus?
We do not come before his table,
hear this call to making peace, go forth
to work and build his peace, alone.

There *is* a real presence,
a presence with us who has also given us
a solemn word of promise:
"Take, eat, this is my body.
Drink ye all of it, this is my blood. . . .
But I will be with you.
Behold, I will be with you
in your family life, strengthening you
to hold back the angry word, the impatient gesture,
the hostile deed. I will be with you
in your working life, guiding you
to ways that will no longer set my people
at one another's throats but will join them,
hand to hand, in cooperation for the good of all.
I will be with you in your political life,
helping you to seek out and support
policies which, while they take notice of
the threats from other powers, do not construct
an entire government, a national way of life,
around the requirements of defense.
I will be with you in your church life,
your community life, building bridges of conciliation
across the ancient chasms of old spites
and grudges. I will be with you even
at the center of your life, making peace within
reconciling all the conflicts, tensions
that can rip the soul to shreds.
I will be with you if you trust in me."

This is the message, therefore,
not only of the burning bush, but of the cup,
the loaf, the common table too—that Christ
has bought, has brought, has wrought our peace.
Now it is up to us to live in it
and share it.
It is a risky business.
Do not let anyone persuade you that
making peace is easy. It cost our Lord
his life just to set the process moving.
But then, we inhabit a risky world, one which
could be ended, any moment, by
the pressing of a button, the throwing
of a switch. The question is,
Which risk do we prefer?
The risk of continuing this present,
even escalating insanity; or the risk
of starting, here and now, to restore the paths
of peace in every corner of our lives?
The promise has been given, has been kept.
The Lord is in our midst, in bread and wine,
in book and benediction and in every act and impulse
toward love that burns like fire in our hearts
and will not cease its burning till
this world is won, and one in peace.

Exodus 3:11

> But Moses said to God, "Who am I . . . ?"

And Yahweh said,

> You shall be called
> the repairer of the breach,
> the restorer of streets to dwell in.

Chapter Four
Genesis 27—28

JACOB AT BETHEL

And [Jacob] was afraid,
and said, "How dreadful is this place!
this is none other but the house of God,
and this is the gate of heaven."
> —Genesis 28:17, KJV

Do you ever feel afraid
when you go to church on Sunday?
Did you ever know real fear
as you entered the house of God?
No, not the mere anxiety of hunting
desperately for a place to park some wet
and windy morning; nor that sudden
flash of panic that the usher is going to
seat you way down front; not even that chill
and slowly dawning dread that the preacher is
about to ask you to dig a little deeper,
give away more of your substance than
you want to, or can afford.
But did you ever feel
honest-to-God afraid in church?
Have you ever known the stark
and quaking terror of the temple of Almighty God?

The kind of thing that Jacob,
waking in the wilderness, arousing from his dream
of the ladder reaching into heaven
and of angels climbing up and down, the voice
of Yahweh telling him of promise for the future
and of presence on the way, the kind of thing
that Jacob felt and responded to
in dread

> And Jacob was afraid,
> and said, "How dreadful is this place!
> this is none other but the house of God,
> and this is the gate of heaven."

Of all the rich and varied themes
touched upon in our contemporary preaching
and theology, one of the most neglected
is the theme of fear.
We preach and write today of love and hate,
of peace and war, hope and despair—but fear,
whether it be regarded as unworthy,
unpopular or unhealthy, fear seems to be
a forbidden topic nowadays.
Look through our worshipbooks and hymnals,
scour the indexes of the theological tomes,
and you will come up virtually empty-handed.
There are, to be completely accurate,
occasional references to things
like awe and reverence; but these
are definitely not the same as fear,
and if you've ever felt real fear
you will agree.

The irony is
that while we Christians are busy
denying or ignoring the existence of fear,
the secular world—the politicians,
gangsters and terrorists, even
the entertainment industry—
are all exploiting this basic human reality
to the hilt.
Whatever happened, then, to fear;
to fear within the context of the Christian church?

> And Jacob was afraid,
> and said, "How dreadful is this place!
> this is none other but the house of God,
> and this is the gate of heaven."

Fear, after all, is a basic element
of life, something we live with, even live by,
almost every day. Without fear
this human race would have ceased
to exist long ago. For fear keeps us
not just from burning our fingers on a hot stove,
but also from burning up this planet in
the final nuclear holocaust (at least,
it has done so far).

37

Fear, to be ruthlessly honest,
accompanies us on every trip to
the doctor's office, every visit to the hospital.
Fear forms a part of every encounter
with someone different from ourselves,
a poor person, an old person, a handicapped person,
a Communist, perhaps, someone
of different color, class or value structure.
Fear travels along with most of us
on every takeoff and landing, every
near miss on the highway, every unaccounted
symptom in our youngsters, every
unexpected prolonged absence
of someone we love, every news report
of a hijacking, terror bomb,
a death by fire, a brutal murder.

Oh, yes, we learn to live with it,
this daily type of fear. We can suppress it.
Often it doesn't even reach the surface
for more than a brief instant, but
it lies there still, submerged.

"I will show you fear in a handful of dust"
wrote T.S. Eliot; and in ten words
says it all. For that "handful
of dust" could be me, or you;
will be, sooner or later, me or you.
"I will show you fear in a handful of dust."
Who can look back
at our history, at this century with
its almost continuous wars and bombs,
revolutions, genocides, famines and floods
and not tremble?

> Like one, that on a lonesome road
> Doth walk in fear and dread,
> And having once turned round, walks on,
> And turns no more his head;
> Because he knows, a frightful fiend
> Doth close behind him tread.*

> And Jacob was afraid,
> and said, "How dreadful is this place!
> this is none other but the house of God,
> and this is the gate of heaven."

----

*Samuel Taylor Coleridge, *The Rime of the Ancient Mariner*,
Part VI, stanza 10.

But fear is not just a reality
in our personal lives, and in the life of
the human race; fear is also a basic part of
our Christian faith. Look back
at the biblical record. Adam's first
recorded words to God, what are they?

Genesis 3:10

> "I heard the sound of thee
> in the garden, and I was afraid."

And this theme of fear before Yahweh
echoes down throughout the history of Israel.
Moses hides his face at the burning bush.
Israel flees in terror from Mount Sinai.
Isaiah quakes before "the Lord
high and lifted up" in the temple.
The psalmist writes,

Psalm 119:120

> My flesh trembles for fear of thee,
> and I am afraid of thy judgments.

Again in the New Testament,
from the fear of those Bethlehem shepherds
who felt "sore afraid," to the terror of Peter
crying out, "Depart from me, O Lord,
for I am a sinful man," to the life of
the early church where we read that

Acts 2:42-43

> they devoted themselves . . . to the
> breaking of bread and the prayers.
> And fear came upon every soul.

We see this same experience
repeated again and again of fear,
trembling in the presence of Yahweh.

And this does not all end
with the last book of the Bible.
The lives of the saints down the centuries
continue to show this same dread experience.
Ephrem Syrus, a monk of the fourth century,
writes of how, at the thought of
God's judgment, he begins to tremble:
"Fear and anguish so penetrate his body
and soul that he begins to moan and groan . . .
his knees begin to tremble
and his very teeth to chatter."
There is Luther's paralyzing terror
at his first consecration of the Mass.
There is Sören Kierkegaard's powerful testament
called simply *Fear and Trembling*.
There is Francis Thompson in luminous stanzas
describing his flight,
"Adown Titanic glooms of chasméd fears,"
fleeing in dread the awful "Hound of Heaven."
Fear, then, both in biblical witness
and in Christian experience down the ages,
is an integral, essential element
in the Christian faith.

41

This said, we have to qualify
this statement. For fear has played
quite differing roles within the faith,
as it has within society as a whole.
Perhaps a major reason we are so wary of
this topic is the way that fear has been abused
in ages past.

> God . . . holds you over the pit
> of Hell much as one holds a spider
> or some loathsome insect over the fire,

preached Jonathan Edwards,
and many more such words in similar
horrific vein. No wonder people wept
and writhed and fainted in the pews back
in those early days. Yet still today
some of our fellow Christians use the same
terror tactics to stampede folk to Christ
like terrified cattle.
This kind of fear is not
the fear of God, it is the fear of hell;
and to employ such brutal methods
to frighten people into faith
is neither truly Christian,
nor is it fully biblical.
And yet, there is a proper
biblical sense in which our God
is to be feared, in which fear itself
can constitute the way to life eternal.

Matthew tells us
at the resurrection that
the women

Matthew 28:8

> departed quickly from the tomb
> with fear and great joy.

The psalmist exhorts repeatedly to

> Serve the Lord with fear,
> and rejoice with trembling.

The apostle Paul,
in that same brief letter
in which he can urge Christians to

Philippians 4:4   Philippians 2:12

> work out your own salvation
> with fear and trembling,

can also charge,

> Rejoice in the Lord always;
> again I will say, Rejoice.

And so it was with Moses and Elijah,
with Peter and with John,
all knew this combination of fear
and yet new faith,
of trembling yet deep trust,
of terror mingled somehow with
the most amazing sense of joy, of
the deepest depths, the most soaring heights
of human emotion brought miraculous together
in an explosive, cataclysmic, life-changing,
world-shattering experience.

43

Might this be why we know
so little of true joy, true faith,
real commitment in our churches,
in our lives today,
because we are unwilling
to face the fear?
Might it be that we
are more afraid of fear
than we are of God?

How often are we alone with our own selves?
Whenever, by some chance, it happens,
the radio or TV is swiftly blaring.
We seize a book to read, a magazine to scan,
anything rather than face the fear,
the fear of being completely alone, and then,
that further fear, the fear of finding
oneself in the presence of the pure,
full, unadulterated and therefore overwhelming
love for us and for all that is God.
Love can be like this.
Love can do this . . . make you afraid.
Love can be a terrible, as well as a
many-splendored thing; because
love not only gives, it seeks, it evokes.
Love yearns for and ultimately
demands a response, the free response
of your own love, and that can be
a fearful thing to ask.

Look what we did to Jesus
when he came to us armed with only love.
We were so terrified by him,
by the questions he asked,
the example he set, the promises
he offered, the kingdom he proclaimed,
that we nailed him to a cross.
We killed him in our fear.
Yes, love can make us fear.

> 'Twas grace that taught my heart to fear,
> And grace my fears relieved,

wrote John Newton, two hundred years ago.

> How precious did that grace appear
> The hour I first believed!

Can we face the fear?
In our Christian churches today,
in our wishy-washy religious ways,
in our bland and moderate,
homogenized, almost anesthetized
twentieth-century daily lives,
can we know once again the terror
and then the triumph of God's judgment,
the grace and glory of God's searching and
redeeming love? This is
the question posed by this fateful,
dreadful, yet immensely hopeful incident
from the book of Genesis.

Perhaps the church
will have to rediscover fear
before it can ever find its way again
to faith and hope and joy.
Perhaps the only way to life itself
leads right through fear
to love.

And Jacob was afraid,
and said, "How dreadful is this place!
this is none other but the house of God,
and this is the gate of heaven."

46

ELIJAH AND THE VOICE

And behold,
there came a voice to him,
and said,
"What are you doing here, Elijah?"
—1 Kings 19:13

So it's "Welcome back once again to Horeb"—
homecoming, so to speak,
at "the mountain of the Lord."
Just two chapters ago we stood here,
on this very spot, or more or less, this Horeb,
Mount of God, and witnessed Moses
talking to and through a burning bush.
Now we find Elijah—
Elijah the hunted, harried, despairing prophet
of Yahweh, standing on this very mountain
to watch his God pass by.
Welcome back to Horeb!

What is it that brings us back
to this forbidding place? Why must we return
all this long way, forty days and nights across
the wilderness to a cold
and lonely cave high up the bleak
and barren face of the mountain?

Permit me to look back a moment, back
to set the scene, back to learn what manner
of man this is that stands in Moses' place
upon Mount Horeb.

The people, Israel, have reached
their Promised Land. They have settled
there and prospered there and got themselves
a king there, a whole series, a dynasty of kings.
Right now they are subjected to the rule
of one, King Ahab, and his lovely,
lively wife, Queen Jezebel.

Under Jezebel's considerable influence,
Ahab has invested the cult of Baal
with the official royal seal.
He has promoted the worship of the old
fertility god of Canaan within Israel,
and the people of Yahweh
are forgetting Yahweh.
They are forsaking "the God of their fathers"—
I Am Who I Am—Yahweh who has led them
out from Egypt, through the desert,
to this fertile, fruitful land,
and they are worshiping the Baal who,
they believe, will make their newfound fields
and vineyards grow and flourish.

48

Jealous for the ancient God of Israel,
Elijah, Yahweh's prophet, summons all the priests
of Baal to a contest on Mount Carmel.
He challenges them to build an altar there
and then to call down fire from Baal
to consume their animal sacrifice.
They try all day, but fail.
At sunset Elijah builds his altar.
He floods the thing with water,
soaks the wood all through,
and Yahweh sends down flame so that
Elijah's sacrifice is consumed.

In triumphant holy rage
Elijah seizes the false priests
and slaughters every one of them
beside the brook on Carmel. Meanwhile,
back at the ranch, or rather in the royal palace,
Jezebel hears of this massacre and vows revenge.

1 Kings 19:2

"So may the gods do to me, and more also,
if I do not make your life
as the life of [these my priests]
by this time tomorrow."

The prophet panics,
flees for refuge in the desert.
So great is his despair and dread that he
asks Yahweh to take away his life.

49

Instead he is sent packing on a journey
to Mount Horeb, Mount of God.
Following in the footsteps of Moses
he climbs the holy mountain, hides deep in a cave,
and there renews his complaint:

1 Kings 19:10

> "I have been very jealous for the Lord,
> the God of hosts; for the people of Israel
> have forsaken thy covenant, thrown down
> thy altars, and slain thy prophets with
> the sword; and I, even I only, am left;
> and they seek my life, to take it away."

What happens next has been the subject
of countless sermons, meditations, hymns,
poetic flights of fancy: how Yahweh passes by
in earthquake, wind and fire,
yet does not speak through any of these,
but only in the still, small voice.
What can this mean, this
still, small voice?

Was Yahweh rebuking Elijah
for his savage, violent measures
against the priests of Baal and urging him
to adopt the ways of gentle persuasion
(a Quaker interpretation!)?
Was God perhaps proclaiming,
"I am not to be discovered within
the world of nature but only in the still,
small voice of conscience"?

50

Or do we see here a historic change
being signaled in Yahweh's methods
of revelation; away from spectacular events
that command the passive attention of the masses,
toward a quiet, personal communion with
the heart of each believer?

Each one of these alternatives
has been put forward many times by preachers
in the past, and they may well be right.
However, it is also possible that much more
is read *into* this old tale than is read out
by such creative musings. The focus
of this narrative is not so much on *how*
Yahweh appeared to that poor refugee Elijah,
but rather on the message, on the words
Yahweh addressed to him.

> And behold,
> there came a voice to him,
> and said,
> "What are you doing here, Elijah?"

"What are you doing here, Elijah,
wandering in the mountains, watching thunderstorms
while my people struggle, life and death,
to resist the cult of Baal? What is this dreary
litany you keep mumbling about altars
cast down and prophets all slain,
even begging me to kill you?
Get up off your knees, Elijah,
I've got work for you to do."

And the Lord said to him,
"Go, return on your way . . . and you shall
anoint Hazael to be king over Syria; and Jehu . . .
king over Israel; and Elisha . . . to be
prophet in your place."

"Go, Elijah, get going,
return on the way you have come."

This also has happened before.
Moses fled the land of Egypt, hunted
as a murderer; and just when he believed
he was safe, Yahweh appeared to him
and sent him back. The God who sends people back,
this One who will not let us
rest in safety or in despair while people
suffer slavery or are led astray, is the God
whom we encounter in the still, small
voice on Horeb.

It's as if you've had
a most disastrous week. The kids
were all sick, your spouse quit talking to you,
the plumbing backed up, the car wouldn't
back up, your doctor told you,
"Slow down or else!"
your boss told you, "Speed up or else!"

52

You haven't slept in days
and stagger into church on Sunday morning,
subsiding into a pew and listening
for the soothing tones of holy music,
when a voice sounds in your ear,
"What are you doing here, Jim or Peggy,
Al or Jane? What are you doing here when my folk
are starving and oppressed, lonely
and in despair? Now get back
to where you came from and do something
about it."
"But what is to be done, God?
These problems are simply too vast,
too encrusted and entrenched for little me
to make a difference."

Take a closer look now
at what Elijah had to do:
"Go back the way you came
and anoint Hazael king over Syria,
and Jehu king over Israel."
Or look again at Moses:
"Go tell Pharaoh,
'Let my people go!'"
These were political acts
that God commanded, actions that were destined
to have profound impact on the fabric of society.
Elijah is ordered to institute
two separate revolutions against
the existing regimes in Syria and in Israel.
Moses is charged to confront
the mightiest empire of his day
and lead a rebellion of its suffering slaves.

Oh! But that would
never do in our day, would it?
Politics and religion, after all,
must not be mixed. How many times
have you heard that? How many times
has it been uttered as an old, accepted truth?
Could it be the phrase originated
on the lips of Pharaoh himself when Moses
told him, "Let my people go"?
"Now Moses, we can't go mixing
politics and religion, you know that."

Yahweh, this God of ours,
if we are to be addressed by these two encounters,
would seem to be deeply concerned
about politics, about government,
about folk who are oppressed, or who are
being led astray after false values
and false gods. But that was
all so long ago, so far away.
Just take a look at what is happening
today, right now, when religion
and politics get all mixed up together.
What about those fellow Christians
in what is called "The Moral Majority"
storming the ballot boxes in the name of Jesus Christ?

Yet, while we may not
necessarily agree with all their policies,
their positions and their tactics,
at least these people are beginning
to take seriously the call to every follower
of Christ to concern about, involvement with,
commitment to this world our God created
and sent the Lord to save.

Another fellow Christian
of our times reminds us all
that Jesus was not crucified in a cathedral
between two candlesticks, but on the town
garbage heap, between two thieves—
in other words, in that place
where the problems and the issues
of our world are inescapable.

Might there not be, even yet,
a way in which some of that revolutionary
openness which has transformed the modern ecumenical
movement might also flower between Christians
of conservative and liberal persuasions;
at least a "Bible-based" discussion
of what Yahweh requires of us together
in the political arena?
Incredible? But then,
we serve a God who deals
in the incredible.

In any case, whatever
our allegiance, left or right or
firmly down the middle of the road,
the God of Moses and Elijah—this God
whom we encounter on the mountaintop of
our own disillusion and despair—
is calling us to action;
action to renew the ways of peace
in a war-torn, hell-bent world, action
to feed the millions around us who starve while
we overeat, action to restore a moral sense
to government, to public life, to business,
schools and churches too.

There are, of course, no
simple answers, no one candidate
or party that can set the whole thing right;
that approach has been tried and has failed too
many times before. This is a task
that will demand the utmost sophistication
and subtlety, all the resources
of our intelligence, our creativity,
our courage and our skill. The Lord we
Christians share found that
it took his whole life, and his death too,
to even get things started. But if he
could die to save this world,
then surely we can live and work as Christians
to heal this world together.

> And behold,
> there came a voice to him,
> and said,
> "What are you doing here, Elijah?"

Chapter Six
Judges 6—7

GIDEON
AT HAROD

And the Lord said to Gideon,
"The people are still too many."
—Judges 7:4

The name of the game,
as everyone knows today,
is success. The whole secret
of life is to win, to seize and hold onto
the victory. From sports to business,
from politics, diplomacy, all of the way
to the grim field of battle itself,
we find this one concern pervading
our thinking . . . how to win big,
whatever the cost.
Now, at last, here in the Bible
of all places, we seem to find just what we need
to support such a view. A tale about winning no less,
an encounter with God that seems to contain
some clear and concise new instructions
on success and failure.

The first thing to strike home
in rereading this story of Gideon
is the stress on reducing the ranks,
the seemingly vital importance of being
under strength. You see it
now and then in sports. A team
runs into a series of minidisasters—
injuries, accidents, illness and the like—
and just when everyone has counted them out
they start playing as never before,
adversity spurring performance
far beyond any previous level.
All this till the team returns to
full strength, then inspiration
evaporates like a dream,
and they fall back upon their old, familiar,
mediocre ways. The importance, then,
this secret disclosed to Gideon,
of being under strength.

Perhaps there is a word here
for the church in these times
when our culture seems obsessed by
the adding up of numbers and statistics,
captivated by the popular mythology
that revolves around the computer,
the calculator, the public opinion poll;
this age when, it seems, everything
that happens can be quantified,
statistically analyzed to death.

The numbers tell against the church,
or so it would appear,
with declines for many years
in church attendance, membership
and Sunday school enrollment,
all the areas the numbers business calls
"key indicators" of success or failure.
The religion boom of new
and shiny steeples in the spreading suburbs
has ground down to a halt, and might
even be described as in reverse.

Yet Gideon's encounter with Yahweh
beside the spring of Harod, this whole
alarming business of the *reductio ad absurdum*,
the stripping down to sheer lunacy
of the host of Israel from
some thirty-two thousand warriors
to a mere troop of three hundred;
this tells us that numbers
are not the most essential thing,
indeed are not all that important in the end.

> And the Lord said to Gideon,
> "The people are still too many."

What *is* important?
What *is* it can be called
essential to the victory?
Look again at the encounter. Here
is Gideon, an inexperienced youth,
summoned from his family farmyard to attempt
the sheer impossible. He is called
to set free Israel (a constant task, it seems),
Israel again a subjugated, apathetic people
with no one left to lead them
in throwing off the hated yoke of Midian.
For Midian has armies thick as locusts,
has camels without number, like
the sand on the seashore.

Gideon, however,
called to action by Yahweh,
emboldened by the testing of God's favor
with the fleece set out by night,
has sent out the ancient rallying cry,
gathered of all the tribes and clans of Israel
thirty-two thousand soldiers to his side.

Not much against so vast a foe;
still, with skilled guerrilla tactics—
no pitched battles, sabotage, hit-and-run
attacks by night among their rugged hills
and valleys—there's no way of telling
what might be achieved in a long
and patient, dogged campaign.

But listen!
What is Yahweh proclaiming now?
What is this crazy Yahweh telling Gideon
to do? "Send them home, Gideon.
You have brought out too many men.
Send them home, or they will think that
they have won it for themselves.
Let every man who is afraid, everyone
who came only because he felt he ought to come,
because all the rest were coming,
everyone whose heart is left back home
with wife and family, and so is liable
to cut and run at the first sign
of possible defeat, let them go now!"
And more than two-thirds,
twenty-two thousand of them left.

> And the Lord said to Gideon,
> "The people are still too many."

The first thing that counts,
don't you see, is commitment—not how many
you have, but how much do they care.
How deeply do they resent the alien boot
of Midian upon their land, their homes,
their necks? How much are they willing to risk,
to lay on the line and then lose,
if need be, in order to win in the end?
The first thing that counts is commitment.

How much do we care?
Do we love the Lord Jesus Christ
and his church just as long as they
make no demands, just as long as
the church is the right place
to be Sunday mornings, just as long
as our pledge can be met without pain,
just as long as no harsh and disturbing questions
are raised about racism, sexism,
justice and prisons, about ethics in business,
marriage and sex, about the misuse of hard liquor
and drugs, about our being held responsible
not just for each other, our own kind,
our children and old folk, but also
for all the lonely, the lost and the starving
who have no one left to care? Is this
the extent of our commitment
to Christ? Is this just as far
as we go for the One who went all the way
to a cross and a tomb for our sakes?

Then stay home!
The church will be better without you.
A harsh word, to be sure.
A severe word of judgment set within
this ancient tale of battle. "Let them go home!"
says Yahweh, "the Lord God of hosts."

For in times like these,
when the vast hosts of Midian,
the principalities and powers of greed
and oppression, ignorance and fear,
threaten the very existence of all things,
our God will need more than
mere Sunday-morning Christians
to carry off the victory
that has been prepared for God's people.

Judges 7:4

> And the Lord said to Gideon,
> "The people are still too many;
> take them down to the water
> and I will test them for you there."

So Gideon took his ten thousand
down to the river to drink. They had
marched hard and long to reach that rendezvous,
and then had stood through all the heat
of that long, tense day awaiting orders;
therefore, at the sight of the water,
they forgot everything but their thirst,
threw themselves down and gulped
great quenching draughts of cool, clear liquid.
However, here and there, along the banks,
a few maintained their vigilance.

These were men who did not forget they were
in enemy-occupied territory, liable
to be attacked at any moment; seasoned warriors
for the most part, who drank slowly
and with care, carrying the water
to their mouths in one hand,
with the other hand firm on the hilt
of the sword.

And Yahweh said, "These!
These, Gideon! These are the ones
I choose to snatch victory out of defeat."
And three hundred men
were left at Gideon's side.
The sports writers today
would call this "intensity";
a kind of fierce, all-encompassing
awareness of the task, the challenge
at hand; an emotional, mental and physical
concentration that will never be caught napping
because it knows just how high are the stakes,
just how vital the prize.

But let's be somewhat careful here.
There are, today, many groups
of highly intense Christians—those
ferociously earnest believers who take themselves
and their beliefs with such utter and deadly
seriousness that they usually succeed
in either terrifying those they meet,
or turning them off completely.

This is not the kind of fierce faith
that this incident is calling for.

Jesus, himself,
had surely the most intense
relationship with and commitment to
"God the Father" that has ever been experienced.
Yet he found time to rejoice in the beauty
of nature—flowers and birds—
the laughter of children,
the wonder of human relationships,
friendships, love.

What this tale demands
is a disciplined life
in the old-fashioned sense of that word.
"Discipline" comes from a root
meaning "pupil" or "student," "follower."
A life, then, that is lived in the study of God,
the steady, sure awareness of God's presence,
God's grace, God's will; this is what is sought:
a life not easily turned aside
into byways of this or that latest pursuit
or pastime, but which moves steadily ahead
through prayer, Bible study,
meditation, daily deeds of witness,
truth, and service, to grow stronger in the One
who calls us to be his disciples.

> And the Lord said to Gideon,
> "The people are still too many."

Commitment, then,
and concentration, intensity,
discipleship, yes; and one more quality.
Now that Gideon has his force
the battle is still to be won.
What is essential now? What else is needed
to rout an army with three hundred men?
Well, at least a sword, a spear
and a shield per man; and armor, all
the protection you can find.
But to creep into that enemy camp
and overthrow it only one thing
could bring them victory, only one weapon
might be wielded with success,
the weapon of surprise.
No clumsy armor must get in the way.
No clattering weapon can betray their approach.
Only a trumpet (probably a ram's horn),
a jar, and a lamp made of clay.
Such weapons to take on a multitude!
And yet, a famous general
once called this book of Judges
"the best guerrilla manual ever written."
The stratagem worked. The surprise
was complete, the panic total.
"The sword of the Lord and of Gideon"
carried the field with hardly
a blow exchanged.
And all through one weapon . . . surprise!

A lone Jew,
a wandering carpenter turned preacher
with his motley dozen or so companions
riding into Jerusalem one morning
on a donkey, no less!
Do you think the Roman Empire,
greatest power in all history till then,
even blinked, even noticed their approach?
Yet, within three hundred years,
that mighty empire knelt in surprise
at the foot of his cross.

Isaiah 52:14-15

> As many were astonished at him . . .
> so shall he startle many nations;
> kings shall [stand agape] because of him.

We his followers today,
have we lost that old weapon, surprise?
In an age that appears so completely foreseeable,
so computer-predictable; a world where
there would seem to be no more surprises left;
an aging, time-weary eon where all
the news is old and stale and repetitious;
can we Christians even yet be surprising?
What if we were to break right out
of all the familiar molds and stereotypes,
the expectations of long centuries
of compromise with power and authority,
and dazzle this darkened world again
with love?

Can we yet sound forth
those ancient thrilling trumpets?
Can we, even now, shatter
the age-old and encrusted jars of fear
and caution, and let the light
of truth shine forth across these
shadowed times? What an amazing challenge!
Not to save the world—the Christ
has already done that for us—
but to surprise it; to shock
this hidebound, crusty old creation
full out of its hell-bound ways, and into
the knowledge and the wonder, the rapture
and the glory of God's grace, God's peace,
God's Reign based upon justice
and on truth. An enormous task!
An impossible task!
But then, this book, this faith, this church
is all about achieving the impossible.

And the Lord said to Gideon,
"The people are still too many."

Chapter Seven
Genesis 3

ADAM AND EVE
IN THE GARDEN

And the man and his wife hid themselves
from the presence of the Lord God among
the trees of the garden.

—Genesis 3:8

Ask, if you will,
the typical Christian congregation
just why they go to church, why they gather
in the peculiar way they do week after week,
why they join, support a church school,
precisely what they believe they are engaged in
in that whole spectrum known as church activities;
ask this, and many would answer
with the image of a quest.
"We are in quest of something.
We are on a common, a shared search
for meaning in our lives, for a purpose
behind all we do, for something vibrant to
look forward to, for intimacy, for communion,
for love, even, yes, a quest for God."

Now there is a valid sense
in which this could be an honest answer,
at least for many. Yet this is also
far from the whole truth of the matter.
At times we are pilgrims, to be sure,
seeking more light upon the way.
But there are other times, it has to be admitted—
many other times, in fact—when this
is anything but the case.

Or, to put the matter
in another way: Think of the Bible.
Many would claim the theme
of this great Book of books is simply this:
The Human Quest for God,
the age-long searching of this race of ours
to see and know and finally be at peace
with that holy ultimate
we call our Maker.
But when we open up the book,
scan its pages, even briefly, we find
that this is not the case. This book is not
about our quest for God. It is, in fact,
the record of God's quest for us.

Look back at other encounters—
Jacob, Moses, Elijah, Gideon—
nowhere in any of these do we read the tale
of someone setting out to seek for God
and finding God atop a mountain,
in a cloud or burning bush.
Indeed we find the opposite scenario.

A person is engrossed in all the daily things
of life and then is suddenly encountered—
encountered by the living God.
It would, in fact, be accurate to say
that our quest for God is, at its very best,
a sporadic, an occasional, a weak and sometime thing;
and were it not for God's unceasing quest for us
we would be lost, forever lost.

> And the man and his wife hid
> themselves from the presence of
> the Lord God among the trees of
> the garden.

This encounter, the meeting
between Adam and Eve and their Creator,
would suggest even more. It would suggest that,
far from seeking God, the characteristic human pose
is one of hiding, of flight from
the divine presence.
Look over the incident briefly
once again. It is toward evening
in the garden of creation.
Over all the beauty of that perfect place,
trees, flowers, living things of all descriptions,
over all that peacefulness there hangs
a guilty silence. The serpent now
is hid among the leaves. The forbidden fruit
lies bitten to the core. Adam and Eve
are trying, frantically struggling
to construct two garments out of fig leaves.

A sound is heard—a sound
of passing loveliness—a sound
that should have filled their hearts
with welcome and with gladness.
It is Yahweh, walking in the garden
in the cool and fragrant breezes
of the twilight, singing, perhaps, a song
of carefree joy in all the gracefulness
of this new-created world, coming now to seek
communion with the man and woman
brought to life to know, reflect God's love,
to share in all this beauty.

They panic at the sound,
dive headlong in the forest,
crouch there trembling, learning
for the first and fullest time all that it means
to be ashamed; but cannot finally resist
the voice that calls, "Where are you?
Where are you?"
So the sorry tale
comes stumbling forth
in guilty, broken sentences.
"I hid because I was naked and afraid."

And the blame is shuffled back and forth.
"*She* gave me to eat . . ."
"I didn't know—the *serpent* tricked me."
"It's all your fault, God,
for bringing me the woman in the first place."
And the consequences follow, as they must,
upon this act of disobedience:
expulsion, exile, punishment and pain,
the final pain of death itself.
In all a simple story. A childish tale,
or is it, rather, child*like*—that is
to say transparent, clear and true,
startlingly true.

> And the man and his wife hid
> themselves from the presence of
> the Lord God among the trees of
> the garden.

We flee from God, do we not,
much of the time, most of the time?
We hide amidst the forest of our days
keeping busy, oh, so busy! with our work,
our precious work, the latest project, that old
ambition, that bright new opportunity.
Even when we are not at work
we still conceal ourselves behind a host
of intricate diversions—seeking pleasure, fun and games,
seeing the world, learning new subjects, creating
artifacts of usefulness or beauty, even
serving others, doing one thousand and one things,

anything at all, in fact, that will protect
us from the presence and the judgment
of our God. We even flee
from God in our experience of dark despair
and cynicism, curling like a hedgehog
into a tight, unseeing ball of sharp defenses
rather than to face the searching love of God.

Why are we so afraid of silence?
We fill up every vacant space and empty moment
with the din of our diversions, our amusements,
our escapes. Even in the elevator or
holding on the telephone the noise
has to be there, prepackaged music to shut out
the presence, to keep us from ourselves
and from the One who waits
within the silence.

"I hid because I was naked," said the man.
And we know precisely what he meant. We share
that sense of nakedness in one form or another.
We all, you see, have things to hide,
forbidden fruits that we have tasted, acts,
incidents, deeds that we have done
or left undone, that we would admit to no one,
not even, fully, to ourselves.

The psychiatrists, the counselors
can tell us of the struggle, the hard
and bitter agony it takes to achieve one tiny
glimpse of openness, of honest sharing
of the inner self.
What, then, must it be like
to face the One who knows us through
and through, the One who sees
to every aspect of our nakedness?

No wonder that Isaiah
and countless others from the scriptures,
confronted by the Holy One,
had to cry out, "Woe is me!
For I am lost . . . !" For God is the One who knows,
knows us even better than we know ourselves,
and we cannot bear this kind of knowing.
So we hide. We do not seek for God.
We flee from God.

> I fled Him, down the nights and down the days;
>   I fled Him, down the arches of the years;
> I fled Him, down the labyrinthine ways
>   Of my own mind; and in the midst of tears
> I hid from Him, and under running laughter.
>   Up vistaed hopes I sped;
>   And shot, precipitated,
> Adown Titanic glooms of chasméd fears,
> From those strong Feet that followed, followed after.*

---

*From Francis Thompson, "The Hound of Heaven."

And the man and his wife hid
themselves from the presence of
the Lord God among the trees of
the garden.

God seeks for us.
We flee and hide from God.
Yet the story does not end in flight
and hiding. It does not even end (did you notice?)
in judgment, sorrow and condemnation.
The judgment is there—has to be there.
No God could be true God who did not judge, condemn,
abhor our foolishness and senseless pride,
our deception and wounding of each other
and of our own selves.
But beyond the judgment there is mercy.
Even in this tale of our first sin the love
and tender care of heaven comes bursting through.
It is a simple gesture, really,
once again a childlike touch,
as God, the Maker of heaven and earth,
having expelled the sinners from the garden,
then sits down and fashions clothes to warm them
and protect them in their exile.

And the Lord God made
for Adam and for his wife
garments of skins, and
clothed them.

We all have seen those bumper stickers
that proclaim, "I Found It!" We all
have heard fellow Christians tell of how
and when they "found the Lord."
Without intent to call in doubt
the genuine sincerity or the honest faith
of those who make such statements, one must still
point out what seems a deep misplacement
in their understanding of the role of God.
We do not "find the Lord." "The Lord" was never lost.
We were the lost, the wandering and astray
on the hillside after dark, and "the Lord,"
our loving Shepherd, has found us,
has sought us out and borne us home
rejoicing on strong shoulders.

God has called us out from hiding;
has judged us, shown to us
the emptiness, the lifelessness of all
our ways and then forgiven us; has set us
on our feet again and sent us on our way
new-clothed in love.
As Isaiah the prophet puts it:

He has clothed me with
the garments of salvation,
he has covered me with
the robe of righteousness.

Isaiah 61:10

77

We do not find God.
Our God finds us and covers
all our nakedness with the mantle
of free grace in Christ our Lord.

A famous German Christian,
Jürgen Moltmann, rediscoverer for our time
of the Theology of Hope, tells, in the story
of his faith, of being taken captive by the British
in February 1945. For three long years
he remained a prisoner of war, learning
in those years of the collapse and ruin of all
that he had fought for, the appalling revelations
of the crimes committed in his country's name—
Buchenwald, Belsen, Auschwitz and the rest.
He fell apart. The deprivation
of his life in prison coupled with the shame
upon his people all but destroyed him
and his fellow prisoners. They felt betrayed,
but also deeply shamed and guilty.

"Then," he writes, "there came
a gradual change." No flash of sudden revelation,
no instant and complete conversion, but a slow,
steady dawning sense of "God's presence
in the dark night of the soul." A prison chaplain
gave Moltmann a New Testament and Psalms.

And there, within those ancient living words
he was encountered,
encountered by a presence and a power
that would not let him sink in the abyss
but held his head up high
above the rising waters of despair, gave to him
the gift of hope, hope amidst the barbed wire,
the hunger and the shame.
"I owe my survival to these experiences,"
Moltmann writes. "I cannot say that I found God there.
But I do know in my heart that it is there
that *he found me*, and that otherwise
I would have been lost."

> And the man and his wife hid
> themselves from the presence of
> the Lord God among the trees of
> the garden.

The message of the scriptures
from their earliest beginning, the message
of the lives of fellow Christians down the ages,
all tell us God is seeking us,
yes, even here and now.

No matter how and where we hide
our God will seek us out, will search us
through and through, stripping away every cheap
and petty power we have tried to build our lives around.
And then will send us forth reclothed,
clad in the shining garments of full mercy,
divine grace, to serve God and
to praise God's name forever.

> And the man and his wife hid
> themselves from the presence of
> the Lord God among the trees of
> the garden.

Chapter Eight
Genesis 18:1-15; 21:1-7

SARAH
AT THE TENT FLAP

> So Sarah laughed
> to herself.
> —Genesis 18:12

I wonder if she knew,
this tough old woman, veteran
of grim decades of wandering through
the desert and the steppes, crouching now
behind the flap of Abraham's tent, eavesdropping,
as was her wifely privilege, upon her husband's
mealtime conversation:
I wonder, did she realize
who it was that spoke this outrageous
piece of nonsense about her bringing forth
a son. A son indeed, at her age!

Three strangers
like these characters
who feasted on her fresh-baked loaves,
the curds and milk and calf's meat
of proud Abraham's hospitality,
might be anybody after all, from merchants
to monastic wanderers begging their bread
from one oasis to the next.
There was, however, something strange
about their bearing, something almost lordly
in their manner of approach;
otherwise how explain
the magnificence of Abraham's welcome—
hardly the "cup of water and a morsel of bread"
he had offered in the first place.
What had happened?

Who might they be?
Ambassadors traveling in disguise, perhaps.
Maybe even kings, three kings come
bearing gifts to grace the birth
of some new royal prodigy
among the city dwellers to the West.
Whoever they might be
they had no business meddling
in her personal affairs.

How dare they talk of children,
prying loose the scab that had, at last,
been formed across that open, bitter wound
between her and her husband?
Had it not been sufficient for her
to have to put up through the years
with all the airs, the haughty,
fertile arrogance of that Egyptian Hagar harlot
and her half-bred son, Ishmael?
And even, long before, to be passed off,
in fright, as Abraham's sister, shoved into
the harem of a foreign potentate just to ensure
that Abraham's neck was spared . . . Had she
not born enough humiliation
without this final, foolish,
cruel insult?

A son indeed! And now,
when all the fun and frolic
of the bridal tent, the marriage bed,
was a poor wistful memory, and she herself
a crooked, dried-up stick, her fabled beauty,
ripeness that had drawn even proud Pharaoh
to her side, now withered into wrinkles,
skin and bone; how absurd the whole thing sounded.
How like, in fact, that crazy God
whom Abraham had followed blindly from
a prosperous, stable home in Haran
to these endless, arid lands where tents
and flocks moved on from year
to year and never settled down.

Yes, maybe that's the one
who is behind this whole mysterious visit;
Yahweh, with those promises of land and sons
and kindred like the starry skies
for number. Poor Abraham,
that doddering old fool, to be deceived again,
to still believe that nonsense after
all these years of endless disappointment.

Well, I'll tell you one thing,
I'm not falling for it this time.
Old Abe can mumble
all the promises he wants to
from his precious, divine Yahweh,
but he won't come near me again.
It can't be done. Just look at me.
It simply can't be done. Why,
the very idea . . . at our age!
It's enough to make you
laugh or even cry.

                    So Sarah laughed
                    to herself.

These patriarchal stories
from the dawn of time do not,
in fact, show women in a fair
or favorable light. Poor Sarah here
seems all too much like Eve, an accessory
or a scapegoat, one who serves, at most,
to portray the more foolish, willful
aspects of our race.

Yet, there is in her a saving grace,
an element that we can all reach out to,
as opposed to Abraham with his faith
austere, supreme. It makes us smile to think
that Sarah laughed. It gives us hope
to know that this mother of all faith,
this one whom Abraham cherished
and who cherished him through thick and thin
could still chuckle at the promises of God.

After all, they are incredible,
are they not? A world of peace when
all around are wars and preparations for
more wars. A world of truth
when lies are the commonly accepted currency.
A world of beauty when the pall
of smoke and smear defaces more and more
of this earth's surface. A world of love
when fear has caught the human heart
within its icy grasp and chills
its every beat to sullen, cold survival.

Yes, we welcome Sarah
in this story with her harsh,
despairing laugh because, if there is room
for her within God's plan, there may be
even room for us who laugh at God
in our time.

We watch someone we care for
droop and die, and hearing the old promises
of life beyond the grave we bow our heads,
but deep within we know a bitter laugh
that says, "This cannot be."
We hear the preacher
soar to heights of eloquence
in speaking of "faith, hope, love . . .
these three . . ." and then we nod and rise
to go, but deep below we hear
that hollow voice that cries,
"Life is not so."
We stand before a sunrise,
listen to the sweep of symphony,
weep and rejoice within the lifetimes
of a novel or a play, yet, all the time,
the laughter calls,
"Things do not work out that way."

1 Corinthians 13:13

                    So Sarah laughed
                    to herself.

Yet Sarah laughed again
when she bore Isaac, son to Abraham.

Genesis 21:6, NEB

          Sarah said,
          "God has given me good reason to laugh,
          and everybody who hears will laugh with me."

For the laughter she had known,
the laughter of deep pain and many tears,
had been transformed beyond all hoping
into new and clean and radiant peals
of laughter in the life
of one called Isaac,
Isaac which means "the laugher,"
"One who laughs."

Some years ago I was permitted
to be present at the birth of my own child.
After all the months
of waiting and discomfort,
after all that long and humid July day
of sweat and blood and even tears I did my best
to share, when she arrived I laughed aloud.
Was it relief, or joy,
or simple wonder at the miracle, astonishment—
who knows? But when she cried her cry
was joined with mine in sudden laughter.

And many, many years before,
another woman heard the messenger
of Yahweh tell her that she was to bear
a son, a son called Jesus, and she said,
in face of all her fears
and future turmoil,

> "My soul
> magnifies the Lord,
> and my spirit rejoices
> in God my Savior."

When the Lord restored the fortunes of Zion,
we were like those who dream.
Then our mouth was filled with laughter,
and our tongue with shouts of joy.

Yes, there is laughter,
honest laughter, in our God.
Ours is not a grim and desperate business,
the survival of the faith at any price;
ours is a faith of freedom, of life
and affirmation, a faith that can
and will transform even the bitter laughter
of despair into the radiant, rippling joy
of birth to life eternal, a faith
that teaches us, through pain at times,
that all the sufferings of this present are not
really worth comparing with the glory
that is held in store for us,
for all in God's design.

This is the word
that Sarah brings to us
in her sad laughter at the door
of Abraham's tent, and in her full
and joyous laughter when God gave to her
a son. This we know through God's own Son,
the child of Mary, child of promise,
child of laughter, Jesus Christ our Lord.

> So Sarah laughed
> to herself.

Chapter Nine
Genesis 22

ABRAHAM IN MORIAH

"God will provide
himself the lamb
for a burnt offering,
my son."
—Genesis 22:8

These Old Testament encounters
have all held a certain kind of fascination
as well as a certain terror;
terror, not only in the awe-inspiring
presence of the Holy One of Israel,
but also in the magnitude of challenge,
the sheer dimensions of the task
that is set forth. But none of them till now
is quite the same as this one: for this encounter
between Abraham and Isaac and the God-Yahweh
is not so much inspiring as it is horrifying—
at least to our twentieth-century attitudes
and understanding.

There is, to be sure,
a definite fascination to this tale;
a mounting drama, a suspense,
which grasps the mind and holds it.
But it is a grim and ghastly fascination
that we feel as we read here
of a father's willingness to sacrifice his child,
to spill his own son's life blood,
for the sake of his beliefs.
If a father acted like this in our time
we'd lock him up, declare the man insane.
Then what is such a horror story doing
within our Holy Scriptures? And what
are we to think of Father Abraham, the hero,
founder, archetype of faith?

To look back,
the specific moment of encounter here
is brief, scarcely described at all.
No detail is provided,
no wind or fire, no cloud or cherubim,
only that voice again, that penetrating voice of God
that calls and says,

Genesis 22:2

> "Take your son, your only son
> Issac, whom you love [It could
> hardly be more specific!],
> and go to the land of Moriah,
> and offer him there as a burnt offering
> upon one of the mountains of which
> I shall tell you."

90

And that's all—the whole encounter.
And Abraham obeys.
There is no argument,
no protest such as Abraham had made
over the fate of Sodom and Gomorrah, contending
with Yahweh so that the cities might
have been delivered for the sake
of only ten just men.
Here, Abraham obeys without a word.
The dreadful deed moves on
in steady, almost solemn silence toward
its savage climax.

Abraham rises early (hoping,
perhaps, thereby to avoid any suspicion,
any apprehension on the part of Sarah).
He cuts the wood, saddles the pack mules,
gathers up his son and servants
and sets forth.
Three days they travel,
three dread-filled days of journeying
with not even a suggestion in the tale of the thoughts,
the plans and schemes that must have raced through
Abraham's mind as mile succeeded
anguished mile.

"Can I not simply flee, refuse to carry
out this vile, inhuman deed? Or what
if I should climb the mountain, build the altar,
set the fire, then plunge the knife into
my own heart, not the precious heart
of Isaac? Surely Yahweh
would not require more than that of me?"
No word of this is spoken.
Yet, in this very silence—
this heavy, dark and eloquent silence—
we can sense the height and depth of agony
even now across the centuries.

They sight the mountain.
Abraham moves, deliberate, to his task.
He leaves the servants and the mules.
He lays the firewood on young Isaac's back,
takes knife and flint into his own old hands,
and the two begin to climb the mountain.

Now, at last, a word is uttered.
Isaac, surely growing puzzled, even
somewhat fearful, turns and says, "My father . . ."
"My father," words that must have pierced
the old man's aching heart. "My father . . ."
Abraham answers, "Here I am, my son."
"Where is the lamb?" asks Isaac,
beginning now to be truly afraid.
Abraham replies,

"God will provide
himself the lamb
for a burnt offering,
my son."

So they went
both of them together.

Both together—father, son—stumbling,
shaking, blindly groping on to the appointed
place of sacrifice.
They roll the stones to build an altar.
They lay the logs in order
carefully prescribed for such occasion.
The boy is tethered—hand and foot,
just as one ties a lamb to slit its bleating throat—
and then is laid across the holy place
in silent, quaking dread.
The blade is slowly raised above the boy,
this lad who is not merely Abraham's son—
the son he loves, the miracle of his and Sarah's
latter years—but is also Abraham's only shred of
living hope, the solitary sign that God
has given to hang on to, his sole assurance
that all the sacrifice, all the years
and wanderings, all the dangers and the trials
have not been in vain, sheer foolishness,
but will result, through Isaac, in richest blessing
for his people and for all peoples of the earth.

93

So the future,
all the future he has lived for,
trusted God for, staked his life,
yes, his eternal life upon, lies bound
before him now, below his trembling,
murder-laden hand. He strikes.
But even as his hand begins to move:

>   "Abraham, Abraham!" . . .
>   "Here am I." . . .
>   "Do not lay your hand on the lad
>   or do anything to him."

"For now I know you trust me even more
than all you love and all you hope for.
Now I know you trust me as no one has ever
trusted me till now. Behold this trust will be
called 'faith.' You will be Father Abraham,
father now, not just of Isaac, but of a whole new family,
the family that lives by faith."

The lad is freed.
The ram is found and slaughtered.
And Abraham calls the place
Yahweh Yireh—"the Lord will provide."
It is a dreadful tale; a tale that has called forth
a hundred explanations, rationalizations
from the scholars, preachers, critics.
Yet it lives, still lives today
in all its power and its dread.

94

It lives today because it deals with life,
not the sweet and basically ordered thing that
stands for life in novels, movies and the like,
but raw life, full and true reality. It faces up
as few other tales in this entire Book face up
to the darkness, the utter anguish,
the sheer bloody, bleak despair, even horror,
that exist and touch on every human life
in one way or another, at one
time or another.

That is not to say
that we have here a literal and simple
explanation for all pain, loss, human suffering.
Most Christians nowadays cannot believe the God
of love, "the God and Father of our Lord Jesus Christ,"
would ever cause a child to suffer
just to test the faith of that
child's parents. No! This darkness, this pit
of human hurt and grief, of genocide
and torture is far beyond all simple explanations;
is beyond any explanation as to who,
and why, and wherefore.
Still it happens.
Little children do suffer,
more than suffer, die. People,
every kind of people
see everything they have hoped for, planned for,
all their future, all their dreams, turned
to dust, to tears and ashes.
Yes, it happens.

... Never morning wore
to evening, but some heart did break,*

Blind chance or accident; human sin
or plain stupidity in the form of drugs
and alcohol; lust, greed, ambition breed
an entire world of carelessness: a world
of chemical pollution, of cancers breeding in
our air, food, water; of casual, daily brutality
and bloodshed spread across our headlines
and TV screens; of warfare building upon warfare,
of calamity. No, we do not need to blame
it all on God. The sources of our
suffering lie closer to home
than that.

But it happens—whatever
the cause. It happens. Life falls in.
Hope and love seem smashed beyond repair
and we are dashed into the pit.

What then?

What then?
What will we do, you and I,
when reality, this undeniable,
inescapable facet of reality touches,
as it will, your life and mine?

---

*From Alfred, Lord Tennyson, In Memoriam, 6:2.

What will we do when all our love,
all our future is snatched away and we are naked
and alone? Will we flee from life, crawl bitterly
into our own shell, or what is left of it,
bewail our unjust fate, curse God
and pray for death to end our misery?
Will we turn on those around us
and seek to drag them with us to despair?
What will we do?

There is another option.
There is another path that opens up.
And here is the true message
of this ancient tale of terror—
those three amazing words,

"God will provide,"

spoken when Abraham's soul, his entire being
cried out in agony, "My son, my Isaac,
my love, my hope, my promise for the future . . ."

"God will provide
himself the lamb
for the burnt offering."

And God did provide.

Here is the constant witness
of this Word of God, this Holy Bible,
sung by the psalmist time and time again,
"I was in the pit, my life an empty shell,
a mass of pain. Yet the Lord heard my cry.
He lifted up my head. Praise the Lord!"

This is the Word proclaimed
out of the very depths of degradation
by that other towering man of faith called Job.

> "Though he slay me,
> yet will I trust in him,"

cried Job of God.

Here is the truth set down by Paul
and Peter and the rest, not from the comfort
of a study desk. Here is one thing to be remembered
and held on to: this Book, these promises,
this testimony was not written down by scholars
in seminaries, wise sages on sabbaticals,
preachers off in summer cottages, but by saints,
slaves, servants, men and women literally in chains,
in dungeons, destitution, hunger, awful deprivation.
Yet Paul can write to us, while under
threat of Roman execution,
"For I reckon that the sufferings of this
present time are not even worth comparing
to the glory which shall yet shine forth
in us. . . . All things [yes, even these that
come upon me now], all things can work
together for good to them that love
God. . . . For I am convinced that neither
death nor life . . . nor any other thing in
all creation can ever come between us and
God's love for us in Jesus Christ our Lord."

God will provide.
God does provide, if only
we have faith enough to take
God's hand into the dark,
to take one step in trust.

> If thou but suffer God to guide thee,
> And hope in him through all thy ways,
> He'll give thee strength, whate'er betide thee
> And bear thee through the evil days; ...
> God never yet forsook at need
> The soul that trusted him indeed.*

It was noted at the outset
that there had been no encounter
quite like this one in its horror,
its deathly stark and grim reality.
Yet, there was one,
centuries later, on another hill
outside a city wall, when the wood
of sacrifice was laid upon another human back,
when one who embodied all our hopes,
"the Son of man, the Son of God," that One
in whom the future of our broken race resided,
hung bleeding on a cross and cried,

> "My God, my God,
> why hast thou forsaken me?"

Mark 15:34

---

*From "If Thou but Suffer God to Guide Thee" by Georg Neumark, tr. Catherine Winkworth.

Yet could murmur with his dying breath
the last clear prayer of utter faith,

> "Father, into thy hands
> I commit my spirit!"

And Abraham told Isaac,

> "God will provide
> himself a lamb
> for the burnt offering."

God will provide.
God did provide. God does
provide for us, this day, in every circumstance,
even the most harsh and bitter, a lamb
for the sacrifice, one who shares our pains,
who bears our weary burdens, who walks
by our side through the valley—
yes, every stumbling step—
until we know ourselves and find ourselves
at peace in God's eternal love and grace.
So let us place our trust right there,
firm in the only hands that will not,
cannot pass away. And let us say with Abraham,

> *Yahweh yireh,*
> God will provide.

100

Chapter Ten
Joshua 5:13-15

JOSHUA
AT JERICHO

And Joshua went to him
and said to him, "Are you for us,
or for our adversaries?" And he said,
"No; but as commander of the army of
the Lord I have now come."
—Joshua 5:13-14

What a strange,
intriguing, almost eerie
little incident this is, tucked away
in a corner of the book of Joshua.
It is the eve of the battle of Jericho.
The host of Israel is encamped all about
that ancient stronghold; and Joshua, the commander,
successor to Moses, walks alone among the battle lines
scouting the lay of the land, forming plans and stratagems
for the assault, searching for ways to breach
the megalithic walls of this apparently
impregnable fortress.
Suddenly, in the half light,
he is confronted by an armed man,
a soldier, obviously, with a drawn sword
in his hand.

Immediately Joshua's sword leaps forth
and the old, old challenge rings clear,
"Friend or foe? Our side or theirs?
Are you for us, or for our adversaries?"
And then that uncanny response,

> "No; but as commander of the army of
> the Lord I have now come."

Nothing more.
No secret plan for the battle.
No reassuring promise of divine intervention.
Only these enigmatic words. Why, it could almost
be a scene right out of Shakespeare—
Hamlet, perhaps, *Lear* or *Macbeth*—
this haunting confrontation between
the leader of Israel and the captain
of the hosts of Yahweh.

Biblical scholars
have, no doubt, their explanations.
Obviously, they might argue, a much more
extensive dialogue between Joshua and the angel
has failed to be preserved here, a conference
in which detailed instructions for the morrow are
passed on to Israel's general.
And they may well be correct; for that
is what Joshua seems to ask for.

> And Joshua fell on his face to the earth,
> and worshiped, and said to him, "What does
> my Lord bid his servant?"

Joshua 5:14

102

But the only instruction he receives
is to put off his shoes; he is on holy ground.

Why not accept this text
as it now stands? Why not view this little incident—
this brief encounter—as complete within itself?
What if the key to this passage
were to be found right there
in that haunting, strange response,

> "No; but as commander of the army
> of the Lord I have now come"?

Joshua's question, as has been suggested,
was an old one: "Friend or foe?
Are you with us or agin us?"
a question as old as warfare, as hostility,
old as the basic need to choose up sides.
It is a question that has plagued the human story
from the beginning to this very day,
"Are you for us or for our enemies?"

We ask it in the Christian church,
have asked it since our very earliest beginnings.
"Are you for Peter or for Paul,
for Apollos, for James and the Judaizers,
for the Libertarians? Which side
are you on? Which group, which camp,
which party do you belong to?"
And the assumption always made is that
the one who asks this question
is on the right side, "on the Lord's side."

So we Christians, for nearly two thousand years,
have slandered one another, attacked
one another, imprisoned, flogged and tortured,
even killed each other, because we knew
that we were "on the Lord's side,"
and all the rest were not.

Read once again those horror stories
of intolerance from the Middle Ages
as Catholics burned Protestants, Protestants
burned Catholics, and both together tortured
and burned the Jews. Why, even those groups who fled
to seek religious liberty, a new beginning
in the New World, were no sooner established there
than they began to turn the very instruments
of oppression they had fled from upon
their fellow Christians, Quakers, Baptists,
Roman Catholics and Freethinkers, all
who differed in the slightest from
their own "divinely approved" forms.

Did they never read the parable
Jesus told about the unjust steward,
where the servant who found mercy from his lord
was finally condemned because
he would not share that mercy with his fellows?
Did they never listen to
The Sermon on the Mount?

Matthew 7:1-2

> "Judge not, that you be not judged.
> For with the judgment you pronounce
> you will be judged, and the measure
> you give will be the measure you get."

There is a strong, severe,
a terrible warning there.

Yet, before we fall ourselves,
into the very trap that we have dug,
let us not condemn those Christians from another,
earlier time when, even to this day, we have
our own sects, our exclusive groupings,
our Christians who believe they are the only ones
to be saved; and then the rest of us
who suspect, and secretly hope that they
will be proved completely in the wrong.

Matthew 7:3

> "Why do you see the speck
> that is in your brother's eye,
> but do not notice the log that
> is in your own eye?"

said Jesus. And when we read these words—
you and I—we nod and say,
"Yes, he is so right!
I know a lot of people just like that."

This question, then,
"Are you with us or agin us?"
This need, compulsion even, among Christians
to be in the right among the chosen few,
in order to condemn all the rest,
this insidious vanity that drives us
to division in the name of truth,
has been, perhaps, the major curse
of all our Christian history.

And Joshua went to him
and said to him, "Are you for us,
or for our adversaries?" And he said,
"No; but as commander of the army of
the Lord I have now come."

But this sickness,
this pathological urge to divide,
is not unique to the church of Jesus Christ.
It permeates the entire human fabric.
The words *Gott Mitt Uns*—
"God With Us"—inscribed on the belt buckles
of the Nazi stormtroopers in World War II
remind us of that whole host
of wars and crusades, bombs,
bullets and battleships that have been blessed
in the name of Father, Son and Holy Ghost,
then used in the fierce belief
the "we are on the Lord's side."
Look at Lebanon today,
Northern Ireland and Iran,
India and Pakistan, Israel and the Arabs;
look wherever there is bloodshed,
devastation and inhumanity,
and there you will find people invoking
the name of God, fighting so-called holy wars
(as if that very phrase was not self-contradictory)
confident that, whatever else may fail,
"the Lord" will lead them on to final victory.

And Joshua went to him
and said to him, "Are you for us,
or for our adversaries?" And he said,
"No; but as commander of the army of
the Lord I have now come."

What, then, could be the meaning
of this strange encounter? Might it somehow
have the very deepest significance that
when Joshua asked the angel of Yahweh
to choose up sides, he answered with
a clear, resounding "No"?
Words from Saint Paul come to mind;
words so familiar that we have
almost lost their message.

Romans 8:31, KJV

If God be for us,
who can be against us?

These are not words of conflict and of conquest,
As many have believed
and preached them in the past,
"With God on our side nobody
can stand up to us, no power
can resist us."
What is actually affirmed is this:
"If God is on our side, then so is everyone else.
If God, the Creator,
the Lover, the Redeemer, the Sustainer of all being
is for us then nothing,
nothing in all of God's creation,
can ultimately be opposed to us."

107

Finally, you see, we have no enemies.
Even the last enemy, death,
has been overcome in the resurrection
of Jesus Christ our Lord.

In saying "No" to Joshua's "Friend or foe?"
Yahweh was not just being mysterious
or cagey, but instead was proclaiming,
"No, I do not choose sides.
Behold I am Yahweh, and I am
on everybody's side."
Or, as Hosea put it long ago,

For I am God and not man,
the Holy One in your midst,
and I will not come to destroy.

Hosea 11:9

The news of the gospel of Jesus Christ
is precisely this—that God is on our side—
not just the Jew's side,
not just the Christian's side,
not just the good people's side,
not just the Americans' or the West's side,
not even just the Scots Presbyterians' side.
God is for us,
each and every living, breathing,
sinning and repenting, loving and hating
one of us. God died for us all,
in Jesus the Christ, to prove it.

As for us,
we were never on God's side.
The crucifixion showed that once
for all. When we had the Lord among us
in the flesh, far from getting on his side,
we thrust a spear into his side,
nails into his hands and feet.
Yet that same Lord,
who bore the awful brunt
of all our pride and fear and vicious hate,
that Lord is still on our side.
He went through death and back again;
back not for revenge, but for reconciliation,
still loyal to us despite all
our betrayal; still caring for us
despite all our rejection; still and forever
living for us and within us, each
and every blessed one of us, if only
we will recognize the truth and accept it,
live it as his universal family together.

There *is*, you see, a battlefield
before us. Just like that ancient
Jericho that Joshua faced, this modern,
secular, cynical society we live in
seems impregnable today with all its powerful,
entrenched defensive structures of apathy,
neglect, self-interest and corruption,
prejudice, ignorance, and despair.

Can we begin to crack these mighty walls?
Can we, the host of Yahweh,
Christians of all stripes and persuasions,
take up together the struggle against evil—
an evil that we recognize at work
within our own lives but which, compounded
in society, is destroying human life, the gift of God?
We will not do it if we fight among ourselves.
But if we can listen to each other,
respect each other; if we can cherish
one another realizing that,
when all is said and done, we are
God's gift to one another, given
to stretch each other's minds and hearts
and souls precisely in and through our differences,
then there is no limit to what God can work
within and through us all together.
Then, indeed, we may begin, with Paul,

Ephesians 3:18-19

> to comprehend . . . what is the breadth
> and length and height and depth, and to
> know the love of God which surpasses knowledge.

> And Joshua went to him
> and said to him, "Are you for us,
> or for our adversaries?" And he said,
> "No; but as commander of the army of
> the Lord I have now come."

Chapter Eleven
Isaiah 6

ISAIAH AT THE ALTAR

In the year
that King Uzziah died
I saw the Lord . . .
—Isaiah 6:1

What a matter-of-fact,
down-to-earth, nuts-and-bolts book
this Holy Bible really is!
Not only does it deal with ordinary,
fallible human folk with all their weaknesses,
their faults exposed;
but this Book of books is also firmly rooted
in the everyday, earthy, and often
bloody stuff of history.

This is not a mystical,
quasi-poetical, soaring treatise
of selected lovely thoughts
à la Kahlil Gibran.

Nor is it a book, or series of books,
that floats across the abstract spheres
of philosophical debate—logic,
metaphysics and all the rest.
When you come right down to it
there is practically no theology in the Bible
either, or precious little of what
the scholars of today would label with
that grand and noble-sounding title.

Instead we have, for the most part,
a record of experience, one thousand,
two thousand years and even more
of rich and varied human experience, set down
and then reflected upon, debated as to
meaning, purpose, ultimate significance,
sung about at times and prayed
about in hymns and psalms;
but, above all else, grounded
in the very stuff, the daily
bread and butter of human history.

Thus it is
in this wondrous vision of Isaiah—
this mystical experience, if there ever
was a truly mystical experience—
which is recounted, set forth
for the reader in completely matter-of-fact
terms. And it begins,
as all such history must begin,
with the date,

In the year
that King Uzziah died . . .

Think of that for a moment.
Imagine that you are setting out
to write the most profound description
ever given of what it means
to be human in the presence of the Divine,
and you commence your account,
"In the year that President Kennedy was assassinated,"
or stranger yet,
"In the year the Phillies won the World Series . . ."

Yet, here again,
we come hard up against one
of the most basic, fundamental assertions
of our Judaeo-Christian tradition:
that God, our God, is the God of history,
Almighty Ruler of all that happens. And that God
is to be found, not in retreat,
or in the distant airy realms of abstract
speculation, but at the heart of the events
that weave our destiny or doom, in
complete engagement with this blood-
and-sweat-and-tears world we all exist in
day by day.

Isaiah 6:1

In the year
that King Uzziah died
I saw the Lord . . .
high and lifted up;
and his train filled the temple.

Here is Isaiah,
in the midst of history,
in the pursuit of his regular duties
as a prophet of the temple at Jerusalem,
suddenly transfixed by the inbreaking of eternity.
At the center of the real,
the daily round and course of things,
he caught a vision of complete and ultimate
reality, of what was actually and eternally going on
right there, right then, at the core of this
outwardly routine moment.

> I saw the Lord . . .
> high and lifted up;
> and his train filled the temple . . .
> And the foundations of the thresholds shook.

Has it ever happened to you?
You go to church,
and all the old familiar stuff begins to happen:
the Carillon, the Prelude, the Call,
the Confession, when, like a lightning flash
at midnight, the beyond breaks through,
you suddenly realize what it is
you have been saying, what
it is you are involved in, whom it is
you have been singing to and praying to;
and then the whole world shudders,
seems about to fall apart around you.

114

And the foundations of the thresholds shook.

Above him stood the seraphim;
each had six wings:
with two he covered his face,
and with two he covered his feet,
and with two he flew.
And one called to another and said:
"Holy, holy, holy is the Lord of hosts;
the whole earth is full of his glory."

What are they, then, these seraphim,
these weird, yet almost human creatures who,
along with angels and their kin,
inhabit stained-glass windows, Bible stories,
and the carved corners of cathedrals?
Do they merely represent the fruits
of overheated, superfertile imaginations?
Or could it yet be true,
in a mode of truth that moves beyond all lines
of fact and fiction, that these mystic beings
represent an order of reality,
a realm of good and godly powers,
which lies without our sight and yet within
our ken, beyond all human comprehension
yet just inside the range of our experience?

Did you ever see an atom,
touch a molecule or neutron, taste
or feel or brush against a gamma ray?
Still these, we are assured,
all permeate the fabric of our being.

115

What then? Might it not be equally true
that when we stand and sing in church
we are not simply making a loud noise in
a strange room to scare away the dark, but we
are joining in the hymn of all creation?
Might we be sharing,
not just with fellow Christians, folk
of God across the globe, not just
with all the splendid, radiant singing trees
and foliage of autumn and the spring,
not merely with the rocks beneath our feet
which Jesus once claimed would themselves
cry out, "Hosanna!" if we humans tried
to hold our peace, but responding to the angelic choir
itself in chanting one to another,

Isaiah 6:3

> "Holy, holy, holy is the Lord of hosts;
> the whole earth is full of his glory"?
>
> And one called to another
> and said: "Holy . . ."

Are they calling to us now?
Are we giving any answer?

Isaiah 6:5

> And I said:
> "Woe is me! For I am lost;
> for I am a man of unclean lips,
> and I dwell in the midst
> of a people of unclean lips;
> for my eyes have seen the King,
> the Lord of hosts!"

How else can we respond,
if we ever once-for-all perceive what
really is going on here—that total, cosmic setting
within which we take our humble place?
If we are given this to see,
then there is only one response that fits.
"What have I been doing all these years?
How could I not have seen before?
My God, what am I doing here?
I am unclean!
My life, my lips, my prayers
have been a lie until this moment.
Woe is me!"

Isaiah 6:6-7

> Then flew one of the seraphim to me,
> having in his hand a burning coal
> which he had taken with tongs from the altar.
> And he touched my mouth, and said:
> "Behold, this has touched your lips;
> your guilt is taken away,
> and your sin forgiven."

What a moment!
What an experience right at the heart
of this dreary, daily world!
To find yourself confronted by the power
that brings all things to being,
that love eternal which creates, sustains,
renews all that has being.
And then to be embraced by it,
yes, loved by it, incorporated into love,
but still remain yourself,
yourself beloved.

Amazing grace! how sweet the sound
That saved a wretch like me!
I once was lost, but now am found,
Was blind, but now I see.*

Isaiah 6:7

"Behold, this has touched your lips;
your guilt is taken away,
and your sin forgiven."

Isaiah 6:8

And I heard
the voice of the Lord saying,
"Whom shall I send,
and who will go for us?"

"Go where, God? Not back
into that dreary, dull and empty world
I loved and lived in for so long.
Surely once I have arrived,
once I have glimpsed beyond the curtain
of the way things seem to be to
the way things really are,
surely there is now no turning back.
I could not live that way again. Nothing
there can ever be the same."

"Whom shall I send,
and who will go for us?"

---

*From "Amazing Grace" by John Newton.

Who will return to the sham
and pasteboard world where my children
live their whole lives through
enslaved to scraps of metal, paper,
plastic; where my people hurt and kill
one another to possess such trinkets;
where my people never look beyond to glimpse
the utter splendor, to catch the sheer eternity
that lies, skillfully curled, in every moment?
Who will go for me to share this vision,
to open people's eyes, to tear away
the lies and the half-truths that bind
and blind my children to their destiny,
to this prospect of abundant life I set
before their feet today and every day?

> "Whom shall I send,
> and who will go for us?"

Isaiah 6:8

> Then I said,
> "Here am I!
> Send me."

Fellow pilgrims,
fellow searchers on the way of truth,
fellow stumblers along that tangled path,
fellow souls who, week by week,
draw within the temple courts of God
yet have never caught this vision,
do you see where we have been
with this experience of Isaiah in the temple?

This is the heart of worship we have looked at.
This is that same reality we reach toward
on Sunday after Sunday morning.
In the awe of God's full majesty,
in singing to God's glory,
in the confession of our unworthiness,
in the communication of God's cleansing grace
in Jesus Christ, our Lord,
in the Word, God's Word, which calls
to service and commitment
and in that faithful, clear response,

"Here am I!
Send me,"

we have traced the course of worship
from the Call until the Benediction.
We have traced this path so many,
well-nigh countless Sunday mornings, yet,
till now, we have never fully shared it in the light
of this vision of the prophet.

But the word
of this great man of God, Isaiah, of this great book,
of saints and sages through the centuries
till now, is this:

that here is what is really happening.
No matter what we see, or choose to see;
"the Lord . . . high and lifted up," or
the tall organ pipes;
no matter what we hear or choose to hear;
the angel choir of heaven, or that noisy person
whispering in the pew behind, we still stand
each time we join in worship
before the throne of judgment and of grace.
The fiery coal is offered for our lips.
The summons comes to each and every one,

"Whom shall I send?"

And the challenge, the responsibility,
the privilege is ours still to answer clear
with all the faith that's in us,

"Here am I!
Send me."

121

Chapter Twelve
Isaiah 40

ISAIAH
AT THE WAY

A voice says, "Cry!"
And I said, "What shall I cry?"
—Isaiah 40:6

We stand
among a conquered,
captive people in a strange,
an alien country. Thousands upon
thousands of them there are, people
taken hostage, uprooted from their native
land, their sacred city Jerusalem,
their lofty and majestic temple, then led
in grim forced march across the barren,
endless wilderness here to Babylon.
Babylon the great, the Imperial City,
Babylon of the hanging gardens, fabled wealth
and vast, corrupting power.

They have been compelled to settle here,
hostages, not for six, nine months,
a year or so, but by this time
for over fifty years; fifty years and more
of exile, deprivation, of captivity
and of despair. Where, then, is Yahweh,
"the Lord of hosts"? What has happened
to our God, "God of our fathers"?
Is God left behind in Judah,
hovering, perhaps, above the ashes
of the old Holy of Holies?
How can we sing Yahweh's song
in a foreign land?

It is the eve,
the preparation for *akitu*,
the great Babylonian New Year festival
when Marduk, supreme god of Babylon,
that massive, gilded,
graven image, will be hoisted up, borne
swaying round the outer walls,
then carried back in triumph into the city
on a Way, a highway straight and new,
specially prepared for the god
of this huge empire as he comes to reclaim
the capital city as his own domain
for yet another year.

Among those working on the Way,
breaking rocks, hauling gravel, spreading
fresh, white sand, is a Hebrew slave—
call him Isaiah—
laboring in the service of a false and foreign god.
Suddenly, his body racked in every joint,
his head swimming with hunger and the awful heat,
his dark eyes blinded both by sweat and tears,
suddenly Isaiah hears a voice, then many voices.
He feels himself transported,
lifted somehow from that blistering ramp into
the very council chamber of Almighty God:
not Marduk, but the God of gods.
And a voice says to him, "Cry!"

"What shall I cry, Yahweh?
What can I cry? All flesh is grass,
all its beauty like the flower of the field.
The grass withers all too soon. The flower fades.
Surely the people is grass. What is the use, God?
What's the use? The cry
has been already given ten, a hundred,
thousand times before.
Leaders, preachers, priests and prophets all
have sounded forth your word.
Over decades, even centuries the call
has sounded forth till now, 'Repent!'
They have spelled out your judgment, Yahweh,
the doom that still is imminent, times
without number. No one listened.

They would not hearken to the cry of Amos,
Hosea, Jeremiah and the rest and now
it all has ended up like this;
your chosen, special people bound in chains
and exile, forced to bow the knee
before an idol made of clay.
Surely the people is grass!"

A voice says, "Cry!"
And I said, "What shall I cry?"

We stand among a conquered, captive people
in a strange, an alien country.
But this time it is not one people,
one solitary victim nation, but a race,
a species, an entire world that is in exile,
captive to forces beyond all control,
fearing to trust, not only their own leaders,
but the very food they eat, the water that they drink,
the air they breathe. They are surrounded,
shut in, captive by the very weapons
set up for their own defense, but which,
if ever used, will surely also bring about
their own destruction. This is
a lost, perplexed, frustrated, fearful people,
a people who bow down to gods,
to many gods, gods of power, of prestige, of property;
gods which, in their heart of hearts, they know
are made of common clay, and can and will
be shattered in the end.
And to these people also
a voice says, "Cry!"

"What shall we cry, Yahweh?
It's all been cried so many times before.
We fought a war, two wars at least,
to end all wars. We created
first a League and then United Nations
to settle all disputes in peace
and avoid the need for bloodshed.
We embraced a form of government by laws
with careful checks and balances. We built up
our churches to reinforce the family,
to teach us how to live together,
to lift the human spirit.
Now look at us, God.
Our families fall apart, our
institutions crumble, or are for sale
to the highest bidder, roller of the dice.
Our leaders act more and more
like characters in a sitcom on TV.
Our churches fight among themselves,
within themselves. What shall we cry?
What, in God's name, shall we cry?"

Isaiah 40:6-8

A voice says, "Cry!"
And I said, "What shall I cry?"
. . . The grass withers, the flower fades . . .
surely the people is grass.
The grass withers, the flower fades;
but the word of our God will stand for ever.

And now that word of God sounds forth,
sounds forth in some of the finest,
loveliest and most moving lines
in all of Hebrew poetry—in all of poetry:

Isaiah 40:1-2

> *Nahamu, nahamu, yomer Eloheykem* . . .
> Comfort, comfort my people,
> says your God.
> Speak tenderly to Jerusalem,
> and cry to her
> that her warfare is ended,
> that her iniquity is pardoned,
> that she has received from the Lord's hand
> double for all her sins.

What word is this, "Comfort,
comfort . . . Speak tenderly to them"?
Surely the prophets, from the beginning
until now, have cried out doom and judgment,
denounced corruption and apostasy, demanded
of the people to "repent before it is too late!"
Can this truly,
can these gentle, wooing words
to the bruised and wounded heart
of a whole people truly be
the word of our God?

Listen once again:

Isaiah 40:3

> "In the wilderness prepare
> the way of the Lord,
> make straight in the desert
> a highway for our God."

128

Not a triumphal, festal Way,
a cultic ramp for Babel's Marduk,
that wobbling, tottering clay carnival figure
of a god, but a road of return and reunion,
a highway through the desert to Jerusalem,
a pathway of promise, of pilgrimage,
and, above all, of hope.

> Get you up to a high mountain,
> O Zion, herald of good tidings;
> lift up your voice with strength . . .
> lift it up, fear not;
> say to the cities of Judah

(the cities of America and Russia, China, yes and Africa),

> "Behold your God!"

"Your God who comes with might
and yet will feed the flock just like a shepherd;
your God whose mighty arm rules over all
and yet can also gather lambs and carry them,
can lead them, gently lead those
that are with young."

> A voice says, "Cry!"
> And I said, "What shall I cry?"

Isaiah 40:9

129

To a despairing, broken people,
a word of promise; to lost and fearful,
frantic men and women, a word of hope—true hope:
hope, not in this program or that one,
not in this human possibility or that one,
although these will all
have their importance later on,
their role to play in the working out of hope.
Hope, first of all,
and above all, in God.
Hope in love, hope, and more
than hope, trust that this great Power
that has created, still creates, sustains
all the wonder and the radiance that surrounds
us in created things, trust that this Power
has never yet failed us, never let us fall,
never yet completely given up on God's own children,
has even promised never to let us go
and has sent the Son, God's only Son,
to live and die and rise again
in hope beyond the grave.

"Faith, hope, love," wrote Paul,
". . . but the greatest of these is love." Perhaps
for Isaiah's time and ours the greatest need
is more than love, is hope—the wings of love
that help love soar and even sing.
Perhaps God's greatest gift
to us is hope.

1 Corinthians 13:13

Isaiah 40:6

A voice says, "Cry!"
And I said, "What shall I cry?"

We all have seen and known,
lived through or, at least, come into
contact with a share of what this world today
calls "hopeless situations."
A child with a terminal disease,
a marriage torn and shredded far beyond repair,
a lifelong career cut short by unemployment,
a life dragged down to living death
by alcohol, addiction, mental illness.
In the thick of crises such as these
there are times, and not a few for most of us,
when we would prefer anything to knocking
on that door, answering that telephone,
opening that letter, stretching
out that hand of friendship and concern.
There are truly times when a voice says, "Cry!"
And we say, "What shall I cry, Lord? All flesh
is grass. All flesh is grass."

Then, time and again, the door
is opened, phone is answered, and we find
(Behold!) the way has been prepared,
the rough places are all being made plain,
and the glory, not our glory, not the glory of
some church or other institution, but the glory
of our God is already in the act of being revealed
right at the crux of all that seemed
most bleak, most dark,
most hopeless.

Now don't misunderstand.
Here is no shallow, pleasing picture
of a magic god, a made-to-measure deity who
delivers, on demand, checks in the mail,
miracles to order, an easy, painless way
out of all life's tragedies.
This is a God who shared and still
does share, in Jesus Christ, our every pain
and weakness, fear and desert of despair;
a God who sees us through,
who is with us in the valley of the shadow,
has a word for us to speak, a hand
for us to clasp and hold; a God
who is, as Paul wrote to the Christians at Corinth,

> the Source of all mercy
> and comfort,

and who, in Christ our risen Lord, can say to us,
"Fear not, for even death itself
will never separate you from me, from my love."

"Wherefore comfort one another with these words,"
as Paul writes later to the Thessalonians, echoing Isaiah's cry,
"Comfort, comfort my people."

1 Thessalonians 4:18, KJV   2 Corinthians 1:3, PHILLIPS

Wherefore comfort one another and seize hold of hope;
hope in the God who can gather all the threads
of our frail hoping, our wistful,
fragile dreams and aspirations, our tenuous
wishes, good intentions, and weave them
tight around a promise and a holy
presence with us; hope in the God who breaks
even the iron bands of death and hell
to bring us hope, to be our hope.
Then go forth yourselves as heralds,
heralds of glad, good tidings to proclaim
to Judah's cities, to every city of this world,
"Behold your God!"

> A voice says, "Cry!"
> And I said, "What shall I cry?" . . .
> The grass withers, the flower fades;
> but the word of our God will stand for ever.

133

Chapter Thirteen
Jonah 1—4

JONAH AND THE CASTOR OIL PLANT

And the Lord said [to Jonah],
"Do you do well to be angry?"
—Jonah 4:4

No, they didn't get the title wrong.
This is not one of those hilarious typo errors
you can find collected in *New Yorker* magazine.
This chapter was not meant
to be entitled, "Jonah and the Whale,"
even though that whale is all
that people ever think of when they hear
the name of Jonah. Take another look
through that old book and you will see
that the incident with the great fish
(the Bible never actually calls
the beast a whale) is not at all the focus
of the message of this book.

135

The fish, in fact, merely serves
the purpose of bringing Jonah back
from a diversion, back again to where he was
at the beginning of the tale—
under orders from Yahweh.

Indeed, despite centuries of speculation
and heated theological debate concerning whether
or not this whole fishy business
could actually and did actually take place;
despite countless plays, poems, and pictures
showing Jonah in the belly of the beast;
the real encounter here—the true
showdown between Yahweh and this
reluctant servant—takes place
not inside a whale but beneath a plant;
according to the Hebrew, most probably
a castor oil plant.
(And if there's one thing worse
than being swallowed by a whale, it just might be
having to swallow castor oil . . .
But that's another story!)
Hence this chapter's somewhat
tantalizing title: "Jonah and the Castor Oil Plant."

And the Lord said to Jonah,
"Do you do well to be angry?"

The basic story
has been told so many times.
Jonah, a prophet of Israel, is told by God
to proceed to Nineveh and proclaim
"the wrath of the Lord" against that evil city.
Now Nineveh was the capital of Assyria—
Israel's ancient enemy and oppressor,
the Nazis of the ancient Near East,
the scourge of other nations, whose soldiers
had the charming custom of flaying
their prisoners alive before
impaling them on stakes set in the ground.
Jonah is to go there and cry, "Doom!"
An interesting assignment, to be sure—
challenging, yet hardly one designed
unduly to lengthen one's life span, or ensure
a peaceful retirement on a pension
at age sixty-five.

So Jonah does what you
or I would probably have done.
He jumps aboard a ship headed in
the opposite direction; flees for his life
to Tarshish. God, however,
is not so easily evaded.

A storm arises.
The ship is almost wrecked.
And poor Jonah finds himself
cast overboard by the panicked crew,
then swallowed up, held captive in the belly
of a sea monster. He prays to God
to give another chance and his prayer
is heard. Three days later he is thrown up
by the fish, back onto terra firma.

There the insistent Yahweh
calls to him again and, in view
of recent events, Jonah decides this time
he'd better do as he is told.
He goes to Nineveh. Proclaims
the wrath of God and then retires
to watch the dire and awful consequences
with a certain anticipatory glee.
But, lo and behold!
the Assyrians repent.
They accept Jonah's message
and from the king on high down
to the very beasts of the field they repent,
don sackcloth and forsake their evil ways.
Yahweh, meanwhile,
seeing this miraculous transformation,
is, presumably, overjoyed and decides
not to destroy the city after all.

And Jonah . . . Jonah is furious.
"After all this fuss;
Tarshish, the storm, the whale and all;
after all my troubles, trials and tribulations;
I might, at least, have been granted
the satisfaction of seeing these wretched Assyrians
stew in their own juice, writhe
and die in agony. But what
does old softy-God do?
What does that bleeding-heart liberal
of a Yahweh come up with? Forgive-and-forget for
the lot of them. And I am left here looking
like a liar and an utter fool. It's enough
to make you want to give up the ghost!"

So Jonah sits and sulks there
on the outskirts of the city. Soon a plant
grows up beside him and shades the angry
prophet from the sun (this is
a parable, remember, not a piece of literal history),
a broad-leaved, shady shrub that makes
Jonah almost happy once again.
But not for long. Next day the new plant
withers, shrivels up and dies; and Jonah
is reduced, once more, to fury
and despair: "It is better for me to die
than to have to live like this."

But God says, "Jonah, you grieve about
the loss of this one plant that cost you
not a thing, yet you cannot understand
why I would be unwilling to destroy
this teeming, busy city with all
its countless inhabitants."
And there the story ends.

What is it about?
It is not about a whale, that much
is clear. Nor is it really
about a castor oil plant, although
that is where the decisive encounter has
its place. This is, instead,
a story about anger, about two
different kinds of anger: the anger of God
and the anger of humanity.

> And the Lord said to Jonah,
> "Do you do well to be angry?"

It begins with the anger of God.

> "Arise, go to Nineveh,
> that great city,
> and cry against it."

It begins with the anger of God.
There is much about this divine anger,
not only here in Jonah, but throughout the
biblical witness, Old Testament and New.

No matter how we try to play it down,
soft-pedal the theme in our supposedly
more advanced, more tolerant, more humane
twentieth century, we cannot open this Bible
and read in it very far without encountering
the wrath of God. It permeates the scriptures.

Should we, then, call this wrath
a primitive conception, an understanding
of God's nature that has nowadays been outgrown
and can be safely left behind,
abandoned as a relic?
If we do, what are we left with?
A God who does not care when the poor
are trampled down, when widows and orphans
are exploited, when the murder
of children and the rape of women
is an everyday event upon our city streets,
when whole nations and races
are subject to slavery and genocide,
when God's own children heap bombs
upon bombs that are capable of extinguishing
life from this planet in one flash.
Is it really better, nicer,
more comfortable to believe that God
does not care about all this,
than to accept God's anger?

Perhaps we need to picture God
as a kind, sweet, indulgent grandparent
who simply chuckles, shakes a shaggy head—
"What will these rascals think of next?"
Or might it be conceivable that,
in view of the state of things, in view
of the massacre of whole villages of peasant folk,
of the brutal economic devastation of entire cities,
of the ways we money-changers have polluted
and poisoned this whole temple of
God's glorious creation, God
might even be a bit provoked?

There is, it seems, a good case
to be made for wrath; a right and proper,
necessary anger to be found in God.
Who *could* see all this, could witness
all our folly and not know anger?
So we begin with the anger of God.

> And the Lord said to Jonah,
> "Do you do well to be angry?"

But now the story moves to
another kind of anger.
The anger of Jonah.

Jonah 4:1

> But it displeased Jonah exceedingly,
> and he was angry.

And again,

Jonah 4:9

> [Jonah] said,
> "I do well to be angry,
> angry enough to die."

142

This is an angry world we inhabit,
a world where resentment and rage bubble
beneath the surface and then explode in violence
and mayhem. Not only is this true
on the national and international scenes,
it is also true in our own lives,
in our homes and in our churches.
A young minister said recently, upon leaving
his first church after little more
than one year, "When I left I did it
very nicely. All decent and in order.
But after I got clear I felt
like joining the Special Forces—
Green Berets—taking a course in demolition,
or even silent killing."

Yes, our society seems civil,
on the surface. We greet each other
with a "How are you?" and when
we part we say "Take care." We affirm
cooperation, community spirit, working together
for the common good. Yet, for many,
deep inside there are frustrations, disappointments,
resentments, festering hurts, jealousies
and envies that burn away below the surface,
can and do result in hypertension,
heart attacks, domestic violence, drug
and alcohol abuse, divorce and sudden death.
Why? Why are we so angry?
Why was Jonah angry?

Jonah was angry
because events did not
turn out the way he said they would.
He was angry because God had had a change of heart
and blessed a people Jonah had good reason
to despise. All this without even
consulting Jonah first. He was angry
because he felt a fool.
God's anger had not performed
according to his prophecy, his precise
prescription, but had, instead,
been transformed by the mystery of grace
into forgiveness. Jonah was furious
because, in order to save himself from
the wrath of God, he had been forced
to lend a hand in saving others also.

> And the Lord said to Jonah,
> "Do you do well to be angry?"

God's anger, then, and Jonah's.
Do you see the difference?
God was angry because God cared,
couldn't bear to watch as people, God's own people,
lost their lives in cruel oppression, wasted
them in foul corruption, couldn't stand
to see them throw away the richest gifts
they had been born with, gifts
of life and truth and freedom.

Jonah was angry because he didn't care,
wanted only to see Nineveh destroyed,
to witness vengeance on the enemies of his people.
God was angry for God's children's sake.
Jonah was mad for his own sweet sake.

Or again, God's anger
was a passing thing, necessary
to bring about repentance, but eager,
yearning to be turned into forgiving love.
This is the constant message of the scriptures.
Jonah's fury was implacable,
unchangeable, so much so that when
he saw no way of venting it, of getting
satisfaction for his rage, he wished
that he might die.

The rabbis teach that
"Man's anger controls him,
whereas God controls his anger."
And again,
"It is the nature of a mortal that
when he is in a state of anger, he is not,
at the same time, in a state of conciliation.
But the Holy One, blessed be He,
when He is angry is ready
for conciliation in the midst of His anger,
as it is said: 'For His anger is but for a moment.
His favor is for a lifetime.'"

Finally, it must be seen
that God's anger—yes, even the wrath of God—
is in the further service of God's love
and subject to the overall supremacy
of compassion. Jonah's anger is the very opposite.
It is based in the absolute rejection
of compassion. Indeed, it is compassion,
God's compassion, that ignites Jonah's anger
in the first place. Jonah, in fact, is angry
because God is not. Jonah is blazing mad
because his mission has succeeded
beyond any wildest dreams. Sin City itself,
Old Nineveh has repented, turned
to God. Jonah is angry because
he cannot bear God's love.

It would be wise to ponder,
meditate a while upon these angers—
Jonah's rage, and God's—
to examine, if we dare, our own anger,
all the daily irritations, as well as
the ongoing, old, familiar frustrations.
It would be wise to ask ourselves,
Who are we angry for, for ourselves
or for other people? . . . to ask ourselves how ready,
how eager is our anger to forgive?
Is it still able to be transformed into
forgiveness, or have we cherished it so long
that now it sticks like tar, has become almost
a part of us, so we can never let it go unaided?

146

Most difficult, perhaps,
we must ask if our anger, cold or hot,
is there to form a defense from God's love;
is, for us, a way of shutting out
the light that hurts our darkened eyes,
of turning back the gift
of life, because that gift would
ask us to be free? Is our rage a way
of holding love at arm's length
just because we realize, too well,
that there is no such thing
as a one-way embrace, that to accept
love means to give it in return?

The book of Jonah, then,
a fishy, cunning, probing story
not about a whale at all,
but about anger and about love; a love which,
as we know in Jesus Christ,
will not ever let us go,
will not be forever rejected, but will woo
us to the end of time to win us
from our petty fusses, fights and furies
for the full and radiant vistas
of eternity.

> And the Lord said to Jonah,
> "Do you do well to be angry?"

Chapter Fourteen
Ezekiel 1

EZEKIEL
AND THE WHEEL

> And [God] said to me,
> "Son of man,
> stand upon your feet,
> and I will speak with you."
> —Ezekiel 2:1

So many of these biblical Encounters
find their setting in a strange, a distant
foreign place, far from the holy city
or the nation, Israel,
the promised land.
Might this suggest that God
is far more likely to confront us on the way,
than to wait until we reach our destination;
that, if we are to be God's people,
then the call is to be pilgrims, not settled
residents within some heavenly enclave
of an otherwise reprobate world?

We stand again on alien soil,
the river banks of Chebar, among
the Jewish hostages exiled in Babylon.
However, this encounter comes
at the beginning of their captivity, long before
the word of comfort to Isaiah at the Way.
We stand on alien soil
as Ezekiel the prophet experiences
this mind-exploding vision.
Indeed, in reading here of clouds
and flashing brightness, wheeling lights
and wings and smoke, a sapphire throne lifted up
above the firmament, one is almost carried off
to that "close encounter" of another kind,
that climactic scene in Steven Spielberg's movie
when the gigantic, kaleidoscopic, alien spacecraft
arrives and hovers over that spectacular finale.

Just what is really happening to Ezekiel?
What on earth, or not on earth,
can be the meaning of this plethora
of images and bizarre symbols?
Some elements of this highly complex vision
are not quite so problematical as others.
The throne, for one, clearly means majesty,
and set, as it is, high in the heavens
it signifies the majesty of God.

Those wheels within more wheels
all circled round with eyes, wheels
that somehow move in all directions, eyes
that see everything there is to be seen,
would suggest a mobile, universal
kind of God; a God who is not rooted
to one city or one nation—
the deity-in-residence of the temple in Jerusalem—
but a God who is also with God's people
in captivity; a God whose throne
rules over mighty Babylon
as well as tiny Israel.

This alone was a startling new development
in religious thought. Ezekiel's vision
told the people that the God
of Abraham, Isaac and Jacob,
of Sarah, Leah and Rachel, David
and Solomon, was also God of all the earth,
the most high God whose wisdom
is all-seeing and whose majesty reigns supreme.

> And God said to me,
> "Son of man,
> stand upon your feet,
> and I will speak with you."

But there is more to this vision,
more than the truth of God's universality.
The very description, with its odd, uncanny
language and its constant and persistent
qualifications—"the likeness of," "the appearance of,"
"as it were"—points far beyond the limits
of any human description whatsoever.
Yet, by this device,
by constantly qualifying his description
with phrases such as these, Ezekiel is trying
to tell his readers something.
He is saying that, in the last resort,
despite all his vivid, crowded,
rich-encrusted imagery—wheels
and eyes and wings—he has been trying
to describe the indescribable.
He has been grappling with the Mystery
that is God.

The writer of the book of Revelation
does the same thing, depicting for us all manner
of beasts and signs and portents because
this too is the closest he can come
to saying what cannot be said, to describing
the sheer mind-staggering majesty
of the presence of God Almighty.

Small wonder that these two,
Ezekiel and Revelation, along with
several other books in similar vein, are not
among the well-thumbed, regularly taught
and preached-upon portions of the scriptures.

We prefer our Bible
and our God today to be more rational,
more reasonable; in that favorite
Presbyterian catch phrase,
more "decent and in order."
Demanding of us, yes, perhaps;
judging and forgiving us according
to some well-planned schema of salvation;
but God should not, surely, be like this,
completely beyond human comprehension
whatsoever. So we tend
to stick with the familiar passages of
the Bible, passages which, if not completely
comfortable are, at least, quite comprehensible;
and the weird stuff, this bizarre,
mind-boggling material—well, we leave
all that alone because we do not,
cannot understand it.

> And God said to me,
> "Son of man,
> stand upon your feet,
> and I will speak with you."

Yet the thing we have to learn here,
the one thing about God that we
twentieth-century Christians need to rediscover
more than any other, is this. There is
in God, and about God, that which
we are not meant to understand,
which we will never understand.

The mystery of Yahweh,
the utter incomprehensibility of God's
divine nature, that is what Ezekiel
came hard up against by that ancient river bank
in Babylon; and that is what we too
must encounter today if we would not strip
our faith of more than half its content.
Are we looking for a faith
as large as life itself—and death—
as vast as this expanding universe?
Or will we be content merely to consult
a spiritual cookbook now and then,
a holy diet plan, yet another
keep-fit daily scheme of exercises
guaranteed to fit us for the life to come?
Is it sufficient for you
to skate across the shallows of existence;
or are you ready, do you dare,
to launch out upon the deep?

We have become so obsessed by answers
and solutions in our Western world.
Life is seen as a vast mystery, spy, or thriller
novel with clues sprinkled here
and there throughout the plot and everything
spelled out, wrapped up, made transparently clear
by the time you turn the final page—
even earlier if you are smart enough.
This image, of course, is true
to some extent. If all you want
from life are answers, you can get them.

154

There are sufficient answers in this universe
to keep all of us, all our computers,
data processors, busy for the next
thousand years, at least.

But, don't you see,
if all you're after are the answers,
if all you're looking for
in the English Christmas pudding
are the silver sixpences hidden here and there,
then you are going to miss
a delicious lot of flavor and of richness;
you are going to have to ask only
a certain kind of questions,
the kind that are amenable to answers
and to proof.

Our industrial society
has done precisely this. We have
done it with enormous success. The heap
of silver sixpences we have found
is almost overwhelming in its glitter
and its weight. This entire scientific,
technological revolution, with its undoubted
benefits, has been achieved by the asking
and the answering of precisely such
questions as can be answered.

There is no intent here to oppose all this.
Such investigation is a legitimate
and noble enterprise of the human mind.

But what about those questions
that cannot be answered, yet persist,
have persisted with us since the beginnings
of the mind? These are what Abraham Heschel
refers to when he writes of
"the treasures of the higher incomprehension,"
questions which, he argues,
even philosophy has given up on
and left, almost entirely, to the poets.

> And God said,
> "Son of man,
> stand upon your feet,
> and I will speak with you."

These are questions
not so much of what things are,
or of how things work, but of why.
Why is there anything at all?
Why am I alive and someone else dead?
Why did the Big Bang bang—if that is how
all this began? Questions, in fact,
that we first asked as a child
before we became sophisticated enough
to set them aside and look
for something simpler, more accessible
to deal with.

Alfred, Lord Tennyson,
wrote these words more than a century ago.

> Thou canst not prove the Nameless, O my son,
> Nor canst thou prove the world thou movest in,
> Thou canst not prove that thou art body alone,
> Nor canst thou prove that thou art spirit alone,
> Nor canst thou prove that thou art both in one:
> Thou canst not prove thou art immortal, no
> Nor yet that thou art mortal—nay my son,
> Thou canst not prove that I, who speak with thee,
> Am not thyself in converse with thyself,
> For nothing worthy proving can be proven,
> Nor yet disproven. . . .*

Despite all this,
perhaps one of the most fascinating
developments of recent years lies in the fact
that, as the scientists, physicists, astronomers
have probed further, deeper into the what
and how of things, with answer
after answer proving not completely satisfactory,
so they too, at last, are beginning
to approach the question, "Why?" and even,
perhaps, "Who?" Who is the power
behind everything that was and
is and ever shall be?

---

*From *Ancient Sage*.

"A riddle wrapped in a mystery
inside an enigma": words that
Sir Winston Churchill used to describe the Russians;
words which, on a larger scale, might well
describe this whole experience of existence.
"A riddle wrapped in a mystery
inside an enigma." Thus, as we return
to this perception; as the certainties
and confidence of the age of reason which
assumed that it was only a matter of time until
we would understand, and thus control everything
that exists, begin to wane, in this late
twentieth century we find ourselves
once again confronted, as was Ezekiel the prophet,
by the eternal presence of ultimate mystery,
by the everlasting power
of the beyond.

> "Son of man,
> stand upon your feet,
> and I will speak with you."

Two responses to mystery are available,
two possible reactions to the realization that,
for all our facts, our data,
our libraries and technologies,
all we have conquered, at the most,
is a chain of tiny islands in the vast Pacific
of the unknown. We can respond in fear,

close up our minds to the very existence of the
beyond, choose to ignore this fundamental fact
of life, that whence we came and whither we go,
no one has ever told the tale. We can
busy ourselves again with
the easier questions, getting by,
moving along crisis-to-crisis, problem-
to-problem until, one day, it is too late
and we are swallowed up in mystery
and lost. We can respond
to mystery in fear.

The second way is not
an easy one. It is to face
the truth that there are questions
to which, for us, there is no answer;
that there are dimensions of reality—
yes, reality, not fantasy—
that are simply unavailable to human
comprehension. It is to face
the fact of mystery unafraid, and one thing more—
to trust it, trust it with your life.

Do you remember how you
learned to swim? Oh, you could go
to the libraries and the laboratories,
learn every single fact there is to learn
about water and its properties, have all the answers
about water right there at your fingertips
and yet not understand it—not really comprehend
just why it is some people sink while
others float so easily.

159

At last you had to trust yourself—
yes, your very life—into that water and
it happened, slowly, laboriously at first, yet
stroke by stroke you found the water
held you up, supported you.

So it can be with mystery—
the mystery of existence, the mystery of pain
and joy, of music, poetry and dance,
of love, of death, of hope beyond the grave.
Finally you have to trust yourself to it,
give yourself up into its hands if
you would discover for yourself
what this ancient Book has told us all along,
that the mystery is good, not only good,
is God, and loves us with
an everlasting love.

An old African proverb
from the Ashanti people asks us,
"How are you going to see the sun
if you lie on your stomach?"
We have spent so long now on our bellies,
flattened out for cover, or counting out the grains
of sand, mapping the grass roots, analyzing
the behavior of the ants and microbe life.

Is it not time to raise our heads
and let the sun, the full, free radiance
of God's love shine on our fearful faces and show
to us the light of God's eternity?
Ezekiel writes:

And when I saw it
(When I was confronted by the mystery of God),

I fell upon my face,
and I heard the voice of one
speaking. And God said to me,
"Son of man,
stand upon your feet,
and I will speak with you."

So let us stand, recognizing
and accepting the mysteries we can
never fully grasp, yet listening still in trust
for the word that comes from the beyond
in Jesus Christ—God's Word—our Lord—
a Word that brings us more than answers,
tell us that the Mystery, whatever else it may be,
means life and grace and hope
for us for ever.

And God said to me,
"Son of man,
stand upon your feet,
and I will speak with you."

161